Praise for *eBay*™ *Strategies*

"I have met hundreds of eBay scholars over the years, but very few are on a par with Scot Wingo. Scot combines an intimate knowledge of eBay and its workings with a healthy level of skepticism and clear thinking. I found his book to be both entertaining and informative."
—*Jay Sencsc*
   Cofounder, JayAndMarie

"Scot Wingo's new book is a *must-read* for sellers attempting to boost their eBay business to the top level!"
—*Bill Bogardus (biggbill)*
   Top eBay PowerSeller

"The insight, clear explanations, and selling methods in *eBay*™ *Strategies* are going to create hundreds, if not thousands, of new Platinum PowerSellers!"
—*Mike Enos*
   Editor, PlatinumPowerSeller.com newsletter

"Scot Wingo is *the* eBay strategist. His depth of insight is unparalleled in the industry. *eBay*™ *Strategies* is essential for those who make their living online."
—*Scott Samuel*
   Founder, Honesty.com
   Founder/CEO, Ethical Technologies, L.L.C.

"*eBay*™ *Strategies* is a must-read for anyone serious about growing their eBay business. I know because the strategies discussed in this book have helped us become one of the fastest growing businesses on eBay."
—*Randy Smythe*
   President/Owner, Glacier Bay DVD (glacierbaydvd)

"The advice provided in *eBay*™ *Strategies* will help any business achieve a fast start-up on eBay. We have used Scot Wingo's strategies to grow our business to a huge volume. His advice is top-notch."
—*Suzanne Hallam (pugster888)*
   Fastest growing eBay seller in Q2 2004

eBay™ Strategies

eBay™
Strategies

10 Proven Methods

to Maximize Your

eBay Business

SCOT WINGO

Prentice Hall Professional Technical Reference
Upper Saddle River, New Jersey 07458
www.phptr.com

PRENTICE
HALL
PTR

Library of Congress Cataloging-in-Publication Data
Wingo, Scot.
  eBay strategies : 10 proven methods to maximize your eBay business / Scot Wingo.
    p. cm.
  Includes bibliographical references and index.
  ISBN 0-321-25616-6 (pbk. : alk. paper)
  1. eBay (Firm) 2. Internet auctions. 3. Auctions—Computer network resources.
I. Title: 10 proven methods to maximize your eBay business.
II. Title: Ten proven methods to maximize your eBay business. III. Title.

  HF5476.W56 2005
  658.8'7—dc22

                                  2004013328

To my kids, Sean and Dillon.

Thanks for putting up with

an eBay-aholic dad who stays up

'til all hours writing eBay books.

CONTENTS

M ore than a million people actively sell on eBay. Of those people, eBay recently reported that more than 430,000 make a full-time living from their eBay business. These numbers are increasing rapidly every month. eBay drop-off centers such as AuctionDrop are opening at an incredible pace. Late-night infomercials on TV now show successful eBay sellers jumping off their giant yachts, purchased with massive eBay profits!

The number of buyers on eBay is increasing as well, with more than 105 million registered global users—45 million of whom are "active," having bid, bought, or sold in the last 12 months.

Even with the growing number of buyers, sellers are finding it more competitive to sell on eBay. Average selling prices across eBay are decreasing. Why? Because each category has sellers who sell more than $50,000 a month. Those high-volume sellers capture large portions of market share, which allows them to buy their inventory at lower prices. They then pass on those savings to buyers, creating a continuing price war among other sellers.

Although sellers compete primarily on price, other factors such as feedback, branding, promotion, and merchandising determine which sellers can easily be found by buyers—and ultimately who makes the sale.

Get Big Fast . . .

Given the competitive environment on eBay, many sellers go out of business because they are simply outsold by their competitors. eBay's stated goal is to make inefficient markets efficient. Unfortunately, as markets—such as eBay categories—become more and more efficient, sellers have fewer and fewer competitive advantages. In fact, in many eBay categories, the only competitive advantage left is size, and with it the ability to source products less expensively than competitors.

So, if you are selling on eBay and want to survive, you have to grow your business rapidly to stay competitive with the rest of your peer group. If you do not, you will not endure the Darwinian nature of eBay.

Unfortunately, until now, there has been no guide describing what to do after you master the *basics* of selling on eBay. This book is that guide. It gives you two tools proven to generate rapidly growing eBay businesses:

1. **Ten very specific strategies you can start using now to scale your business.**

2. **A framework called the *Five P's,* for thinking strategically about your eBay business. The Five P's are *price, product, promotion, placement,* and *performance.***

Using both of these tools, you will be able to take your business not only to the next level, but also quite possibly grow it into a million-dollar-a-year venture.

Where Do the Strategies Come From?

I am the founder of a company called ChannelAdvisor. At ChannelAdvisor, for the last five years we have helped businesses of all sizes sell on eBay. We provide the software and services that power businesses of all sizes: from individuals with very small operations to large, homegrown firms such as GlacierBayDVD (the largest DVD seller on eBay) to corporate retailers such as Best Buy, IBM, and The Sharper Image.

While working with more than 3,000 eBay businesses, we have developed the strategies and the Five P's framework and tested them repeatedly, improving them along the way. In fact, the strategies in this book drive most of the million-dollar-a-month sellers on eBay—and a large percentage of the million-dollar-a-year eBay businesses, too.

We decided that these strategies are too important to share with just a closed group of sellers; the whole community should benefit from them. So, we compiled the best, most proven strategies into this book.

In fact, throughout the book, I prefer to use the pronoun *we* rather than *I*, because I cannot take credit for creating these strategies, and because *we* more accurately communicates the reality that the content of this book was created by a *team* of more than 60 folks working very hard for the last five years. I'm fortunate enough to be the person who has gathered all of the best practices here in a format that I hope you feel is easy to understand and digest. I hope you come back to the book again and again, as you try the different strategies.

Is This Book for You?

If you want to take your eBay business to the next level, *eBay™ Strategies* will give you the foundation to build on. If you want to develop a million-dollar-a-year eBay business, this book will save you a great deal of time and effort getting there.

Because of eBay's competitive nature, if you're a seller and you *don't* want to grow your business, you will most likely be forced out of business or, at best, forced to change categories every year or so. Even if you don't want to scale your business, this book will help you carve out a niche that will be more sustainable, using the strategies outlined here.

Prerequisites

This book, *eBay™ Strategies,* was designed to be the book you read *after* you've read the basic "how to" books about eBay. So that we can focus on more advanced topics, we've assumed that you have a general knowledge of selling on eBay. For example, you won't find any screen shots of the "Sell Your Item" section of eBay. You should already understand the basics of the eBay auction process, the different listing options, and the after-sales process. In parts of the book, we do recap some areas in which you may be rusty, such as the various eBay listing upgrade options and the fee table.

If you don't have general knowledge of selling on eBay, look first to the excellent on-site help and tools provided by eBay itself. Also, we recommend one of the many "how to" books about eBay, such as *The Official eBay Bible* (Gotham Books), *Starting an eBay Business for Dummies* (Wiley), and *eBay Hacks* (O'Reilly).

Features

You can read this book from cover to cover, and it's a useful reference. Beginning in Chapter 4, each chapter ends with a real-world case study that not only introduces you to an interesting eBay business, but also illustrates the concepts of the chapter and how that eBay seller has leveraged the strategy.

Each chapter contains a detailed summary, so that 3, 6, 9, or 12 months after you've read the book, if you want to brush up on a topic such as pricing, you can read the few pages of summary in Chapter 4 for a refresher. Think of them as Cliffs Notes for *eBay™ Strategies.*

The book also introduces a good bit of terminology that may be new to you, which you will need as you scale your eBay business. All of the important words and phrases are defined in-line in the text, and they are reviewed in the chapter summaries. What's more, all the important terms we define in the text are also gathered in the glossary near the end of the book. So, if you can't remember a specific term, there are three places where you can find it.

Beyond the Book

As you know, selling on eBay is a fluid, ever-changing business. That is part of the fun. With this in mind, we are offering two supplemental, Web-based resources to readers of the book.

First, a dedicated blog (short for "Web log") is available at:

http://ebaystrategies.blogs.com

Here you can get daily updates about eBay, the topics covered in this book, and other items of interest to eBay sellers.

Second, we believe strongly in the concept of community; it's one of the cornerstones of the eBay experience. So, we've created an "eBay group" specifically for readers of this book, where you can ask questions, meet your fellow readers, discuss your successes and failures, and share any new strategies that might be developed. The eBay group is available at:

http://groups.ebay.com/forum.jspa?forumID=100006604

Acknowledgments

First, I want to thank everyone at ChannelAdvisor. Though I'm the author of the book, I'm basically sharing all the fruits of your hard work on behalf of our customers. It's a pleasure to work with such a team of energetic, intelligent professionals. Thanks for all of your input on the book and for all of the eBay best practices you've captured over the years.

Next, thank you to all of the eBay sellers who agreed to participate in the book directly and indirectly, including JustDeals, CrazyApe, Urban Import, Designer Athletic, GlacierBayDVD, MobilePC, Callaway Golf Pre-owned, The Sharper Image, 47st photo, Grapevinehill, MicroExchange, RockBottomGolf, and Transport Logistics.

Finally, thanks to my awesome publishing team—Karen Gettman, Elizabeth Zdunich, Robin O'Brien, John Fuller, Tyrrell Albaugh, Kourtnaye Sturgeon, and Chris Keane—for supporting the project and for all your hard work.

Get Started!

Buying this book is the first of many important steps toward growing your eBay business- and making sure that your business will be around for the long haul, not pushed out of the marketplace by the thousands of new sellers entering eBay every day.

I sincerely hope that each and every one of you finds the strategies in this book helpful to your business. May you blow away your expectations (and your competition)!

Scot Wingo
June 2004

eBay™ Strategies

ONE

Why Build a Great eBay Business?

About a year ago, a friend told me his son had started an eBay business and would really appreciate some advice. As CEO and founder of ChannelAdvisor, a company that helps businesses of all sizes sell on eBay, I am frequently asked for advice on selling on eBay. I'm glad to give it to anyone who'll listen, so I agreed to meet the teenager and see what I could come up with.

The majority of eBay sellers view eBay as a hobby or as a great way to convert their unused possessions into cash. Many also view selling on eBay as a way to support a buying habit (usually collectibles). So, going into the meeting, I was expecting to be asked for tips on how to sell baseball cards or old Star Wars toys or something of that nature.

Much to my surprise, here was Michael, a junior in high school, who wanted to build a million-dollar eBay business. I have to admit I was quite shocked, because most sellers don't start out talking about their goal to be a relatively major seller. I asked Michael the normal questions and found out that he'd started selling on eBay somewhat by accident. He was into customizing his car (like the ones in the movie *The Fast and the Furious*) and had purchased a race car seat for his imported car. The seat didn't fit, and he couldn't return it, so a friend suggested he sell it on eBay. Michael was shocked when the seat sold for 20% more than he had paid for it!

The next day, he went back to the local auto parts store and bought two more of the same seat—and this time he left them unopened. They sold for 25% more than what he had paid. This continued until, by the time he met me, his dad's garage was packed from floor to ceiling, front to back with race car seats that Michael had traveled the state buying and was in the process of selling on eBay. His monthly sales on eBay were in the $4,000 to 8,000 range, and he was wondering how to get them to $100,000. Michael was clearing enough to pay for his first and second years of college, and his father, who had initially been skeptical, finally believed that Michael was on to something.

Michael's questions were straightforward but very advanced for someone so young and so new to the business of selling on eBay. Most of his questions concerned topics such as these:

- **Scale.** Michael wanted to grow big fast, but he didn't know how to grow into new categories. He also felt that his operation was so inefficient, he would have to hire a person for every $4,000 per month in sales.

- **Inventory management.** When an eBay business starts to grow, the most frequent symptom of poor inventory management is selling the same item twice. Another common problem is thinking you've sold everything and having to do frequent physical counts to re-inventory.

- **Product.** Michael had found a product source that was unreliable at best, and he wanted to know how better to acquire product and expand into different categories of products.

Michael also had many issues with logistics, such as shipping, listing items, handling customer support, and more.

I spent several hours with Michael and walked him through the top methods and strategies we have developed at ChannelAdvisor for scaling eBay businesses. At ChannelAdvisor, we manage the eBay businesses of more than 60 large brand-name companies such as Best Buy, Sears, Harman/Kardon, IBM, and Motorola. We also provide software solutions to another 3,000-plus eBay sellers. In total, more than $30 million a month in transactions passes through our software and solutions. To help sellers scale, we've developed frameworks that enable eBay business owners to structure how they think about their business, how they manage it, and how to continue scaling it.

Six months later, Michael e-mailed me to say he had implemented many of the recommendations and had doubled his eBay business. Additionally, he was moving out of his father's garage (his dad was ecstatic about parking his car out of the rain again) and looking to hire several people to help keep up with demand. Michael also had secured exclusive distributor relationships that guaranteed he would not lose his source of product and opened up his business to many new types of product. In fact, Michael's eBay business was doing so well he decided to take a year off before starting college.

Who This Book Is For

For many, eBay is an entrepreneur's dream: the opportunity to be your own boss, set up your own shingle on the Internet, and retire early. In fact, eBay states that more than 430,000 sellers make a living off of eBay. This book is for eBay businesspeople like Michael, people looking for the information and tools to help scale their eBay business and achieve their goals (and dreams) while surviving the very competitive nature of eBay.

Whether you are just getting started selling on eBay or have been at it for years, you will find the concepts presented here will help you maximize your eBay business. If you're not selling on eBay today, this book will save you literally months of missteps and will serve as a reference to which you will come back frequently as you encounter new challenges to growth. Even if you don't aspire to have a million-dollar eBay business, this book will allow you to *sell more* with less effort and improve the health of your current business.

However, this book is not a step-by-step guide to selling on eBay. Countless other books cover that topic in detail. In fact, the features and support eBay provides are sufficient to get a business up to several thousand dollars a month.

In this book, we've captured and collected the best practices of more than 3,000 of eBay's biggest businesses, as encountered by more than fifty marketing professionals over the last four years.

Get Big Fast

At the end of my first meeting with Michael, I asked him why he aspired to have a million-dollar-a-year eBay business; he was already doing pretty well. Michael said, "Well, if I don't grow to be that big in my category, someone else will and they will put me out of business." Michael had come to this conclusion because *he* had driven several competing sellers out of the business of selling the same products. In very little time, Michael had cornered the market for race car seats on eBay.

Michael was right on target with his sense of urgency to get big fast. After working with a large population of eBay sellers over the years, we've seen one thing over and over: On eBay, only the strong survive.

Before we explore why, let's look at what we call the *eBay Economy,* so you will have a basic understanding of the environment in which you are now or might soon be competing. This concept of the eBay Economy explains why eBay is so very competitive and why getting big fast is critical to building a sustainable and profitable eBay business.

The eBay Economy

Since its inception, eBay has grown at a torrid pace, no matter what metric you use. In fact, eBay's well-publicized success is the reason so many entrepreneurs choose eBay when they start their online business.

To understand how to build a big eBay business, it's important to grasp the fundamentals of how eBay works, how big the eBay Economy is, and how great the opportunity is for your business.

Users

The key ingredient to eBay's success is users. Users can be buyers, sellers, or both. Though eBay doesn't categorize its user numbers into buyers and sellers, the overwhelming majority of eBay users are buyers; a relatively small percentage are sellers (estimated to be in the range of 0.5 to 1%).

Since its beginning, eBay has attracted 95 million registered users. Figure 1.1 illustrates eBay's registered user growth over the last six years (as of the fourth quarter, 2003).

In addition to registered users, eBay also regularly reports *active users*. An active user is someone who has bid, bought, or sold in the previous twelve months. For the same period that eBay had 95 million registered users, 41.2 million were considered to be active.

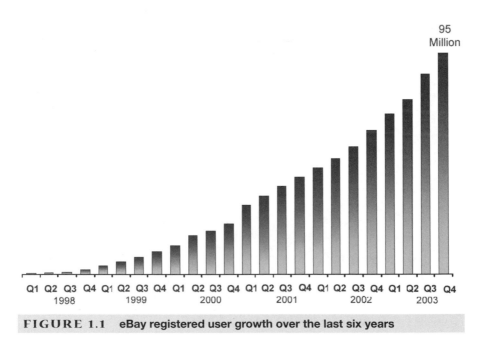

95
Million

| Q1 Q2 Q3 Q4 | Q1 Q2 Q3 Q4 | Q1 Q2 Q3 Q4 | Q1 Q2 Q3 Q4 | Q1 Q2 Q3 Q4 | Q1 Q2 Q3 Q4 |
| 1998 | 1999 | 2000 | 2001 | 2002 | 2003 |

FIGURE 1.1   eBay registered user growth over the last six years

Listings

As you know, eBay sellers list their items for sale. So, eBay's listing metric is an important indicator of how much activity is being generated by eBay sellers. In the fourth quarter of 2003, eBay had 292 million listings (an average listing lasts seven days); there were 971 million listings over the course of the year in 2003. Figure 1.2 shows eBay's listing growth over the last six years.

In later chapters, we will cover how to use this and other information as a strategic advantage.

> **N O T E**
>
> For those interested in monitoring eBay's listings on a daily basis, the site below has daily, weekly, monthly, and annual graphs that are not sanctioned by eBay:
>
> http://www.medved.net/cgi-bin/cal.exe?EIND

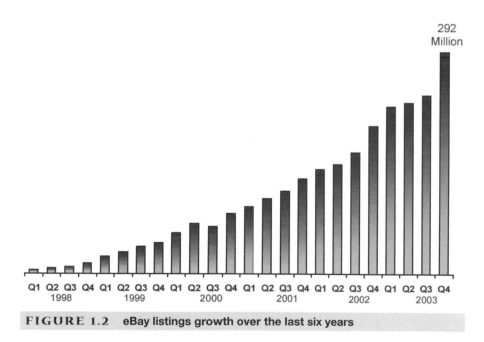

FIGURE 1.2   eBay listings growth over the last six years

Gross Merchandise Sales

Gross merchandise sales, more commonly known as GMS, is the measure of the value of goods that transact in the eBay marketplace. When a listing closes with a winning bidder, then the amount of the winning bid is added to the eBay GMS for that time period. As of the end of 2003, eBay was on a pace of $7.1 billion per quarter (yes, that's a *b*, not an *m*, on that number). In 2003, $24 billion worth of goods transacted through eBay, and eBay started 2004 with a plan to exceed $32 billion in GMS across all of eBay.

Figure 1.3 shows the eBay GMS trend for the last six years.

Categories

Within eBay, goods are separated into a variety of categories. At the beginning of 2004, eBay announced that ten

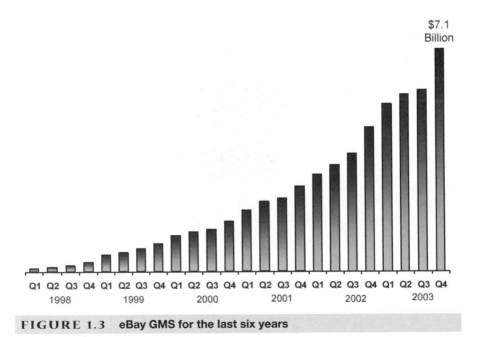

FIGURE 1.3 eBay GMS for the last six years

categories generate more than a billion dollars a year in GMS. Table 1.1 details the categories and their annual GMS run rates.

If you are a seller in one of these categories, you can see the size of the opportunity of this marketplace, or the on-going liquidity there for the taking. For example, in the sporting goods market, there is $1.8 billion worth of goods being purchased a year in that category on eBay. How much of that market can you address with your eBay business?

Sellers

eBay does not publicly release the number of registered sellers or active sellers. However, you can think of eBay's GMS as the total aggregate sales of all eBay sellers.

> **N O T E**
>
> The Nortica eBay 500 (http://nortica.com/UserArea/) lists the top 500 eBay sellers, based on feedback. This site has not been approved by eBay.

TABLE 1.1   Annual GMS run rates on eBay, by category

CATEGORY	GMS RUN RATE
eBay Motors	$7.5 billion
Consumer Electronics	$2.6 billion
Computers	$2.4 billion
Books/Music/Movies	$2.0 billion
Clothing and Accessories	$1.8 billion
Sports	$1.8 billion
Collectibles	$1.5 billion
Toys	$1.5 billion
Home and Garden	$1.3 billion
Jewelry	$1.3 billion

International Sales

Even if you plan on selling only in the United States, it is important to keep an eye on eBay's international operations, because they significantly affect the health of eBay as a company. At the beginning of 2004, eBay attributed more than 33% of its revenues—and correspondingly its GMS and listings—to international sales.

eBay operates marketplaces in more than 27 countries. After the United States, the top four largest countries for eBay are Germany, United Kingdom, Canada, and Korea.

Given eBay's very broad geographic reach, we have seen many eBay businesses seeking to grow rapidly or feeling that they have peaked in the U.S. market capitalize on the international market. They have found that adding an international shipping option can result in a rapid 10 to 20% increase in sales, with minimal effort and additional cost.

Payment Metrics

Since acquiring PayPal in July 2002, eBay has also started releasing detailed information about PayPal usage, called *payment metrics*. A couple of the key metrics to follow are the *total payment accounts* (TPA)(or PayPal registered users) and the *total payment volume* (TPV), or the amount of GMS that goes through PayPal (including PayPal payment volume both on and off eBay).

At the end of 2003, there were 40.3 million total payment accounts and $3.7 billion in total payment volume for the fourth quarter.

It's also interesting to compare the PayPal numbers to the corresponding eBay numbers. For example, the ratio of TPV to eBay GMS has been accelerating, which points to increased PayPal adoption. In the fourth quarter of 2003, the ratio of TPV to GMS was $3.7 billion to $7.1 billion, or 52%.

Other Facts about the eBay Economy

There are literally thousands of other statistics that eBay releases quarterly. Here are a few that are important to consider as you build an eBay business:

- At the beginning of 2004, *28% of eBay's GMS comes from fixed-price sales* versus 72% from auctions. Note: Fixed price includes fixed-price listings, BIN listings (more on these later), eBay Store listings, and Half.com. eBay's fixed-price business alone is larger than Amazon.com's total sales in 2003.

- eBay hosts more than 150,000 stores.

- It is widely reported by the stock analyst community that eBay's average selling price (ASP—more on this later) is in the range of $50 to $55.

- It is also widely reported by the stock analyst community that eBay's *conversion rate* is in the range of 50 to 60%. Conversion rate is the percentage of listings with a winning bidder.

- eBay's *take rate* on average is approximately 6%. Take rate is the percentage that eBay makes from GMS on average in revenue (this includes listing and final value fees). PayPal increases this amount by approximately 3%.

In later chapters, as we dig into the key metrics of an eBay business and how they impact your success, we will reexamine the averages on eBay and provide more background on how these metrics are calculated. And we'll show how they are all interrelated.

eBay Makes Inefficient Markets Efficient

Meg Whitman, eBay's CEO, frequently says that eBay is an online marketplace that makes inefficient markets efficient. One of the most famous economists and philosophers, Adam Smith, wrote copiously about markets. One of his conclusions is that in a perfect (that is, superefficient) market, sellers' profits are minimized and buyers get the best deals possible. Do you think eBay is an example of this?

In reality, as eBay gets larger and more sellers enter the market to sell to the increasing number of buyers, a great amount of pressure is exerted on product prices. Thus, competition on eBay can be fierce. eBay also creates a Darwinian environment, where the strong businesses get bigger and the weak get smaller; eventually only the strong survive (with some notable exceptions, which we will dig into later).

Consider two sellers of any similar item, say digital cameras. Let's call them SellerA and SellerB and assume they have the same sales rate at the start of this theoretical exercise. It's also important to understand that during a given period, there is a fixed number of buyers looking to buy a digital camera, and they will choose between either SellerA or SellerB and assume that each seller has good market prices (compared to non-eBay sources such as Amazon.com).

Now assume that SellerA decides to be aggressive and starts to list more items for sale. The buyers of digital cameras are more likely to see SellerA's listings over SellerB's simply because there are more listings (the listings will also be more distributed over time).

Because of the wider exposure, SellerA starts to sell considerably more than in the past and is now able to buy in larger quantities from his supplier, which in most situations results in lower bulk prices from the supplier. SellerA can pass a big chunk of these "cost of goods" savings on to buyers, thus giving SellerA a more appealing price. SellerA now increases the rate of listing again to support the increased amount of sourced product. Sooner rather than later, SellerA will be orders of magnitude larger than SellerB.

What's worse for SellerB is that SellerB is now in a price crunch *and* a buyer crunch. In addition to SellerB's listings being harder to find because they are obscured by SellerA's listings, SellerB's prices are higher than SellerA's. Buyers will be drawn away from SellerB to SellerA, and eventually, if SellerB does not grow in parity to the rapidly growing SellerA's business, SellerB could be forced out of the eBay digital camera business. SellerB's other option is to match SellerA's prices and make less or zero profits to attract some of the buyers back.

This example may seem far-fetched, but this exact situation is happening every day on eBay today. In fact, here's a real-world example. Take a best-selling digital camera such as a Canon PowerShot S400 and search for it on eBay. Figure 1.4 shows the results.

On this particular day, there are 367 listings for this search. Also, notice that some clever eBay business advertises based on the "Canon PowerShot" keywords (more on this later). For this specific search, we have taken all of the listings and determined all of the sellers for this particular model of camera. When you remove all of the accessories and focus on the digital cameras, there are 179 cameras and 62 unique sellers.

What is interesting is the distribution of the listings across these sellers. The largest number of items offered, by seller, are:

1. **Goodies2001**—31 items (17% of listings)

2. **Imagecam**—25 items (13%)

FIGURE 1.4 Sample results of "Canon PowerShot S400" eBay search

3. **Sunshineelec**—12 listings (6%)

4. **Priceritephoto-com**—7 items (4%)

5. **Topchoicedigital**—6 items (3.5%)

Every other seller (there are 57 other sellers) has fewer than three items. Many other factors help determine the success of a seller, but in this example, the sales of this camera model are distributed across these sellers in a pattern similar to the number of items.

In other words, these five sellers, whose items add up to 45% of the items for "Canon PowerShot S400," will grab 45% or more of the market for this very specific digital camera. Given competitive pricing, the top five sellers with the best merchandising will outsell the others.

Another way of looking at this is that a very small percentage (5 out of 62, or 8%) of the sellers grab a large percentage of the market (almost 45% in this example). You may have also heard this called the "80/20 rule." On eBay, the 80/20 rule is alive and kicking (that is, 20% of the sellers do 80% of the business), and in some very competitive markets (competition increases with liquidity), there is a 90/10 rule and even a 95/5 rule at play.

Whether you have been selling for a while on eBay or just starting, hopefully this example serves as an eye opener and a wake-up call.

The bottom line is that if you do not grow your eBay business into one of the top sellers in your category, the chances of your survival are relatively low.

But Not All Large eBay Businesses Are Great . . .

Even if you are successful in building a large eBay business, a great deal of risk remains. In fact, recently several high-profile top sellers have gone out of business or "flamed out" due to a variety of common reasons.

The problem is, when you start to grow really fast, you push the envelope of your business model, logistics, inventory system, and product sources. Also, relying on high-risk strategies such as selling everything starting at $1.00, no reserve, can be an Achilles heel that eventually brings down an otherwise successful eBay business.

Perhaps the highest-profile cautionary tale is the eBay business Priceitwholesale. In late 2003, eBay profiled Priceitwholesale in testimony before the House Small Business Subcommittee, as well as in many publications:

> Entrepreneur Joe Edery is one of eBay's greatest entrepreneurial success stories. Mr. Edery, owner of Priceitwholesale, which specializes in the sale of cameras and electronics, has had more than 30 years of experience in the industry. Starting in a Manhattan showroom, the idea of using the Internet—more specifically eBay, to expand Priceitwholesale's customer base was very appealing to Mr. Edery. Only after 10 short months, Priceitwholesale led all sellers with an estimated $1.43 million in gross monthly sales. Mr. Edery expects an annual goal of $10 million in eBay sales alone. "eBay is the place where we trade. There's no other source. This is going to be our focus," Edery explained. Priceitwholesale now averages 1,000 to 1,200 listings a day with listings expected to increase.

NOTE

An eBay term frequently used when someone is kicked off the marketplace is *NARU*, which stands for Not a Registered User—the status given to eBay members when they are removed.

Unfortunately, in February 2004, Priceitwholesale stopped selling on eBay and was soon kicked off the marketplace due to excessive negative feedback.

Figure 1.5 shows the Priceitwholesale feedback at the time of their suspension from eBay.

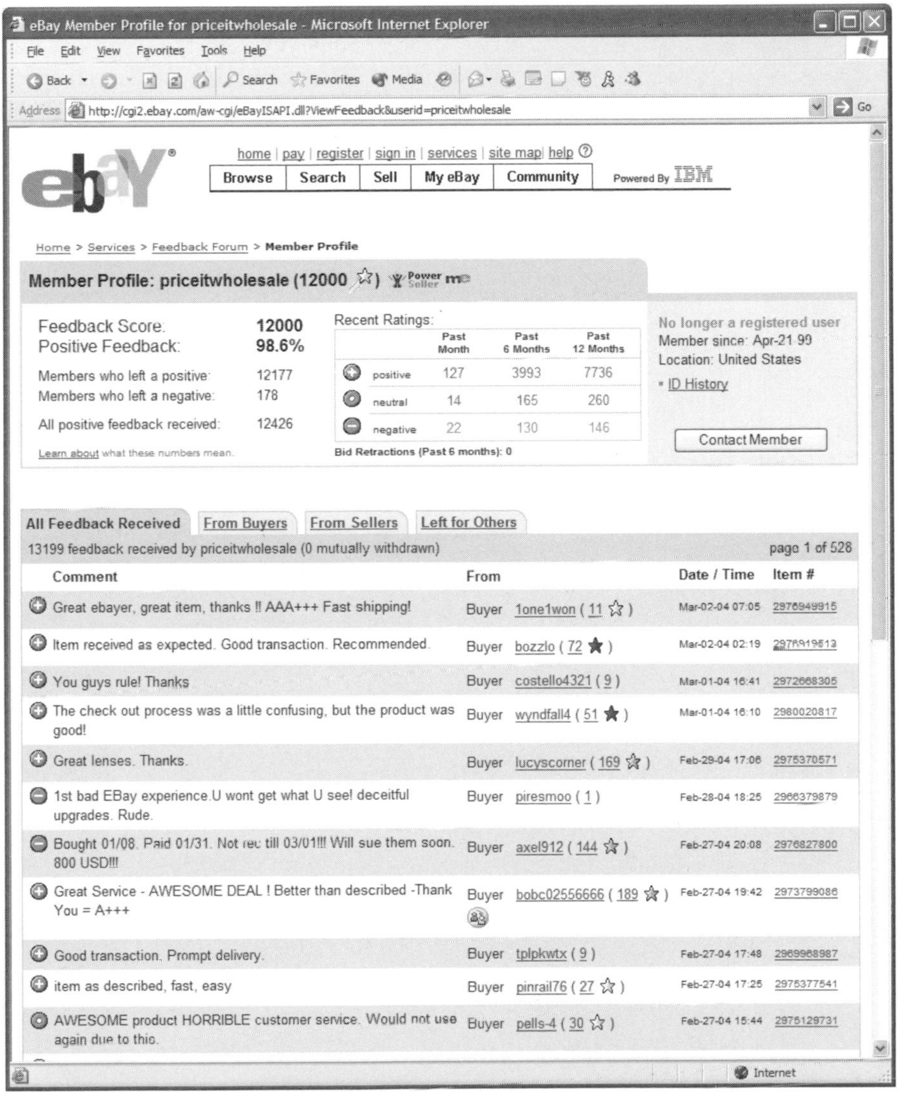

FIGURE 1.5 Priceitwholesale: no longer a registered user

What would cause a seller doing over $1.4 million a month in GMS to accrue negative feedback so rapidly and go out of business? The most frequent causes of flameouts we have seen are these:

- **Strategic error.** Many sellers on eBay use only one listing strategy: $1.00 with no reserve (abbreviated $1NR). This is a very risky selling strategy and frequently results in what we call a "death spiral." The death spiral occurs because once the seller gets larger and lists 10 to 50 of the same item a week, they drive down their average selling prices. This causes them to list more items to maintain revenue and absolute margin, which drives prices down further, ultimately deteriorating margin to the point that the business cannot be sustained.

- **Broken business model.** Some eBay sellers rely on broken business models to succeed in the short term, but they ultimately fail in the long term. The most common example is selling product at a loss on eBay and then making up the revenue by forcing or hard-selling upgrades when the buyer pays. Another common broken business model is to mislead buyers into thinking they are buying a certain product and then to send them something similar, but different. For example, many sellers offer plasma televisions and then ship buyers a kit with instructions on how to build their own plasma television. There is usually some brief mention that the item is a kit rather than a real TV.

  Returnbuy is an example of a business using a broken model. The company would buy open-box returns from retailers such as Circuit City or manufacturers such as Palm, grade them, and then sell them on eBay as is. The company spent over $20 million in venture capital and realized that they were selling the items for less than what they paid, plus the cost of the labor to describe and grade all of the as-is products.

- **Unreliable product source.** Historically, some large eBay businesses have gone out of business or scaled back considerably because their product source "dried up." Usually these businesses are getting their product from unapproved sources. When the manufacturer discovers their unapproved product being sold on eBay by unapproved resellers, they use the eBay VERO program to shut down the resellers. This most frequently happens in the clothing and accessories category and occasionally in consumer electronics. For example, Gucci is very protective of their brand and will shut down any seller that they detect trying to resell goods unauthorized by Gucci.

- **"Presales."** Another famous (infamous) seller, calvinsauctions, not only flamed out but also is under investigation for more than $250,000 in fraud. This company's business model was to "presale" hundreds of laptops every couple of weeks at $NR and then order them from Korea in bulk for the best pricing. The term *presale* refers to the fact that calvinsauctions did not have the computers on hand, but rather sold them before they were made or purchased. Eventually this scheme caught up to calvinsauctions and the firm was not able to ship hundreds of thousands of dollars of items to many eBay buyers.

> **N O T E**
> In many cases, flameouts are caused by more than one of these problems at the same time.

- **Lack of inventory control.** One common challenge arising from selling a large volume on eBay is inventory control. When an eBay business is selling hundreds or thousands of items a week, mistakes can easily happen, such as selling the same item twice, three times, or any number of times. When such problems occur, customers get very upset and generate a lot of rapid negative feedback. The complaints can make your business appear fraudulent in nature to other buyers and even to eBay. Nearly every eBay business with sales of a million dollars or more per year occasionally suffers from this problem.

- **Unscalable logistics.** Some eBay businesses grow faster than their logistics systems (such as fulfillment, invoicing, and accounting) can handle. The result can be hiccups that cause delayed shipments, lost orders, and the dreaded negative feedback.

The good news is that with some forethought and planning, all of the cited causes of flameout (and more) can be avoided, so that not only can you build a large eBay business, but also a very healthy one as well.

The Goal of This Book

This book aims to provide you with the strategies you need to become a top seller in your category as quickly as possible without driving your business into the ground. The book will give you a strategic framework that will guide you to this goal, as well as ten very specific strategies you can start utilizing immediately.

We've shown that only the strong survive on eBay, but what if you don't want to be a top seller? If you choose not to scale your business, this book will give you techniques for creating a defensible niche on eBay, which can protect you from the competitive market forces that are putting many formerly successful eBay sellers out of business. You will also be able to maximize your business and enjoy greater profitability for less work.

How to Read This Book

This book was designed for you to read from cover to cover and then to use as an ongoing reference for your eBay business. The book is built on the concept of the forest and the trees. The old adage "You can't see the forest for the trees" is very important when building an eBay business. In fact, many eBay businesspeople get so involved in the details ("Should I do BIN or fixed price??!") that they don't look at the larger picture of their business.

This book supplies a detailed framework for maximizing your eBay business called the Five P's strategic framework. This framework lets you look at the big picture of your eBay business. In other words, this framework helps you see the forest and to make sure it is healthy.

In Chapter 2, we introduce concepts you will need to build a solid eBay business framework. Then in Chapter 3, we introduce the strategic framework at a high level. Each component of the strategic framework is examined in Chapters 4 through 8, including case studies that highlight a real-world seller and how they have utilized each piece of the framework. Finally, in Chapter 9, we present a comprehensive case study for the entire framework.

Along the way, we highlight ten very specific strategies within the framework that you can implement immediately to increase your eBay business.

For readers who have only a couple of hours of free time and want to scan the highlights of each chapter, and for those who want a refresher after reading the book, each chapter concludes with a summary highlighted in gray.

Finally, for quick reference, the Five P's strategic framework is printed on the inside of the book's cover.

After reading the book, if you would like to learn more, you are invited to visit the book's online blog at:

http://ebaystrategies.blogs.com

Or for a more interactive experience, we welcome you to the eBay group at:

http://groups.ebay.com/forum.jspa?forumID=100006604

If for some reason this URL doesn't work, you can get to the eBay group on eBay by following these steps:

1. **From ebay.com, click on "Community."**

2. **Under "People," choose "eBay Groups."**

3. **In the search box titled "Search Groups by zip code or key-word," type "eBay Strategies" and click on "Search."**

This will take you to the group.

Chapter 1 Summary

NEW TERMINOLOGY

Gross merchandise sales (GMS) — The transactional volume that goes through eBay.

Average sales price (ASP) — The average price an item sells for on eBay.

Not a registered user (NARU) — eBay slang used when a seller is kicked off the marketplace.

Registered users — The total number of registered accounts at eBay.

Active user — A registered user who has bid, bought, or sold in the last 12 months.

Total payment accounts (TPA) — The number of registered PayPal accounts.

Total payment volume (TPV) — The transactional volume that goes through PayPal in a given timeframe.

$1NR — eBay seller slang for a listing that starts at $1.00 with no reserve. Sometimes you may see "$NR" as well.

Flameout — eBay seller slang for when an eBay business goes out of business.

KEY CONCEPTS

The eBay Economy. eBay provides a fertile environment for building a business. Some of the key metrics at the beginning of 2004 are:

- *More than $7 billion in transactions a quarter (that's over $2 billion per month, or about $80 million a day!)*
- *95 million registered users, of which 41 million are active*
- *More than 292 million listings a quarter (or about 100 million a month)*
- *10 categories that produce more than $1 billion in sales a year*
- *40.4 million total payment accounts, through which $3.7 billion a quarter was processed*

Get big fast. eBay's already large and growing size creates a very competitive environment. In fact, if you do not grow your eBay business

Chapter 1 Summary

into one of the top sellers in your category, the chances of your survival are relatively low. However, given this rule of thumb, if you don't wish to be a top seller, you can still take steps to protect your niche in the eBay marketplace and build a defensible position.

Watch out for flameouts. Many eBay businesspeople who initially are able to scale their businesses are unable to maintain their size or growth rate. There are many reasons behind why these companies flame out—all of which are avoidable by understanding them and planning ahead.

The role of this book. This book provides you with the strategies you will need to competitively scale your business, but without flaming out. Once you reach your desired size, the strategies can be employed to protect your market and defend against competitors eroding your sales and market share. The book also introduces a strategic framework that will guide you through the biggest, most strategic decisions you make in your eBay business.

FOR MORE INFORMATION

http://investor.ebay.com
eBay's investor relations site, which contains more information on the eBay Economy.

http://www.medved.net/cgi-bin/cal.exe?EIND
An unauthorized site that tracks eBay listings on a daily, monthly, quarterly, and annual basis. This site also provides conversion rates by category and for eBay overall.

http://nortica.com/UserArea/
An unauthorized site that lists the top 500 eBay sellers, ranked by feedback rating (including country of origin).

http://ebaystrategies.blogs.com
An ongoing discussion and reader forum for topics introduced in this book.

http://groups.ebay.com/forum.jspa?forumID=100006604
An interactive forum where you can discuss topics covered in the book with the author and other readers.

T W O

Building a Foundation for Your eBay Business

The first step toward growing your eBay business is to build a strong understanding of the drivers of every eBay business, as well as the ability to measure them. Even if you are already very sophisticated at measuring your eBay business, don't skip this chapter, because this book's definitions of various measures may be different from yours. Like the foundation of a house, this chapter introduces ideas we will build on in the rest of the book, so it's important that you become familiar with these foundational concepts.

eBay Listings Terminology

As eBay has grown, many new types of eBay listings have been introduced, which can make it very confusing to discuss basic eBay measurements, because each type of listing can affect the measurement.

For the purposes of this book, there are three major types of listing:

- **Auction listing**. An eBay listing with any kind of bidding component. Note that these listings show up in the eBay search engine. Durations of listings vary from one to ten days.

- **Fixed-price listing**. An eBay listing that is fixed price only: no bidding is allowed. Note that these listings show up in the eBay search engine. Durations of the listings vary from one to ten days.

- **eBay Store listing**. An eBay listing that is fixed price only and is available only in an eBay Store. Note that eBay Store listings do *not* appear in the eBay search engine. Durations of the listings vary from 30 days to "Good 'Til Cancelled" (GTC), which auto-reposts every 30 days.

> **NOTE**
>
> eBay has many exceptions that tend to vary by category. For example, listings in eBay Real Estate and eBay Motors are slightly different. For the purposes of this book, we focus on the core of eBay—that is, those categories based in the United States, excluding eBay Real Estate and eBay Motors.

When auction listings have multiple quantities, they are called *Dutch auctions*. Dutch auction bidders enter a quantity in addition to the amount they are willing to pay per item. At the close of the auction, eBay counts the quantities of the top bidders and awards winner status to the bidders whose quantities are within the total listed by the seller, from highest bid to lowest. The price the items are awarded is the price bid by the lowest bidder.

To make life even more interesting, auction listings can also have a fixed, Buy It Now (BIN) price. A buyer can stop the auction by "BINing" the item immediately, without having to bid or wait for the listing to end.

eBay Fees Refresher

Fees charged by eBay have two basic components: listing fees and final value fees (FVFs).

1. **Listing fees**. Also known as insertion fees, these are the basic fees charged by eBay. These prices are tiered, based on the starting price of the listing. However, eBay Store listings are offered at a substantially discounted listing fee.

2. **Final value fees**. The fees charged when an item successfully sells. See Table 2.1.

> **NOTE**
> The most important thing to know about listing fees is that they do not guarantee a sale. You are paying for your item to be on the marketplace *regardless* of whether it sells or not. Thus, if you put too many things on eBay that don't sell, it can dramatically increase your eBay fees. The listing fee structure also benefits you if you start your bidding lower.

Listing fees start at $0.30 (for items that start in the $0.01–$0.99 range) and go up to $4.80 (for items starting at $500 and up). There are numerous optional listing fees, such as BIN, highlighting, featured, gallery, bolding, gift icons, and more. Each of these should be considered carefully, because when your business scales, you need to make sure you are getting a good bang for your eBay buck. We will evaluate optional and promotional listing upgrades later in the book.

TABLE 2.1   eBay final value fees

FINAL VALUE OF ITEM	FINAL VALUE FEE
$0–$25	5.25% of the final value
$25–$1,000	$1.31 (which is 5.25% of the first $25) + 2.75% of the final value over $25
$1,000 and over	$1.31 + $26.81 + 1.5% of the amount over $1,000

Put another way, when you sell something on eBay, your fees are 5.25% of the first $25, 2.75% of the next $975, and 1.5% of the amount over $1,000.

Reserve auctions also have relatively steep listing fees: that is, 1% for items with a reserve of more than $200.

For example, assume SellerX lists three items:

> **N O T E**
>
> Note that the eBay FVF schedule motivates you to sell items at a higher average sales price, because the percentage drops at those levels.

1. A CD with a starting price of $0.01 that sells for $10

2. A laptop that starts at $0.01 and sells for $600

3. A laptop that starts at $500 and sells for $600

The eBay fees can be calculated as follows:

ITEM 1

- Listing fee: $0.30

- FVF: $0.53 (5.25% × $10)

- Total fees: $0.83 ($0.30 + $0.53)

ITEM 2

- Listing fee: $0.30

- FVF: $17.12 ($1.31 + $15.81)
  Note: $17.12 = $1.31 + (2.75% × $575) and remember that
  $1.31 is the 5.25% of the first $25

- Total fees: $17.42 ($0.30 + $17.12)

ITEM 3

- Listing fee: $4.80

- FVF: $17.12 (same as Item 2)

- Total fees: $21.92 ($4.80 + $17.12)

N O T E

eBay fees are a moving target. This
section is meant as an overview
only; you should check ebay.com for
an exact current eBay fee schedule.

As you will see in later chapters, your eBay fees are one input into your strategy, which is ultimately driven by your business model.

Know Your eBay Business Critical Vital Signs

Whenever you go to a doctor, the nurse checks your health by taking your vital signs, such as temperature, blood pressure, heart rate, and so on. In this section, we introduce the *eBay vital signs* (or eBay vitals). Just as when you go to the doctor, your eBay vitals will help you quickly determine the health of your eBay business. We separate them into two types of vital statistics: critical and noncritical. Your critical vitals are the handful of metrics that quickly give you a picture of your eBay business's health. Your noncritical vitals are important but secondary in nature to the critical vital signs.

At eBay seller gatherings, it's always interesting to hear folks discuss their businesses. Usually sellers share some performance data for the first 10 minutes and then spend the next 50 minutes and more describing how they measure the data. Ultimately, it has been our experience that nearly every seller on eBay measures his or her business differently. Thus, when you try to evaluate eBay businesses, it's like comparing apples and oranges. Sure, they're both fruit, they both have seeds and grow on trees, but those are about the only similarities. Unfortunately, there's no standard eBay business vocabulary or reference guide to help all sellers find themselves on the same page.

To solve this growing problem, this book's goal is to create a set of eBay vitals and a corresponding dictionary to formalize the various terms that are currently not well defined.

Don't panic! Although you will need some math to calculate your eBay vital signs, even mathematically disinclined people should be able to get by with a simple calculator and some patience. On the other hand, if you are a math whiz, then you can take many of the vitals to an entirely different level and look at their rate of change, build spreadsheets for measuring them, and so on.

Gross Merchandise Sales

The first and arguably most important eBay vital is *gross merchandise sales,* or GMS. Some eBay sellers call this their eBay revenue, gross sales, top-line, income, and other things. This book uses the term *GMS* because eBay has standardized on the term and reports their own GMS to Wall Street. If you think about your eBay business the way eBay thinks about their business, it will help you immensely to speak the same language if you ever find your-self in a discussion with someone from eBay.

Usually, GMS is measured over a period of minimally a week and on a monthly, quarterly, and annual basis.

Take this example: A seller of CDs and DVDs on eBay over the course of January sells 1,000 items for total sales of $10,000. The seller's GMS is $10,000 for January. Note that the GMS does not include items that are started (listed) in January and close in February. Those items would be included in the February GMS number. In other words, all GMS is captured in the month the item *sells*. Conversely, in this example, some of the $10,000 GMS may have been listed in December of the prior year, but it counts in January because that's the month the item was *sold*, not *listed*.

One important variable that can change GMS is your non-paying bidder rate, described in the next section. We define gross GMS as the GMS without taking into account your NPB rate; net GMS does include your NPB rate. Shipping and handling fees, insurance, and any taxes are not considered in GMS.

Non-Paying Bidder Rate

Unlike normal shopping-cart-based e-commerce, on eBay, when a bidder or buyer wins an auction or purchases an item, he is able to pay later, using a variety of payment methods. On eBay, the separation of buying/winning and then paying results in some sales that appear to be sales but are not true sales, because the item was never paid for and never shipped to the buyer. Buyers who do not pay are commonly referred to as *non-paying bidders* (NPBs). Another slang term you may have heard is *deadbeats* or *deadbeat bidders*. At the time of writing, eBay is even considering renaming them as *unpaid items* (UPI).

We'll call the percentage of such transactions on a dollar basis your *NPB rate*. NPB rates range from less than 1% to as high as 20%.

For example: SellerX's GMS is $10,000 per month. $200 of the GMS was not paid for over the course of the month. In this example, SellerX has the following vitals:

- **Gross GMS is $10,000 per month.**

- **NPB rate is 2% ($200/$10,000).**

- **Net GMS is $9,800 per month.**

Immediate Payment and NPB

Although eBay allows you to recover your eBay fees for an NPB, business owners can spend significant amounts of time dealing with NPBs. Also, an NPB causes your inventory to sit longer, and you effectively lose what would have been a successful transaction.

eBay has introduced a concept called *immediate payment,* sometimes called *immediate buy.* Unlike normal listings, immediate payment listings do not end until the buyer has paid via PayPal and the payment has been confirmed.

Immediate payment can drive down your NPB rate, but it is available only on auction listings that have Buy It Now prices. There are other requirements: the seller has to have a certain type of PayPal account, for example. Figure 2.1 shows what an immediate payment looks like on an actual eBay listing.

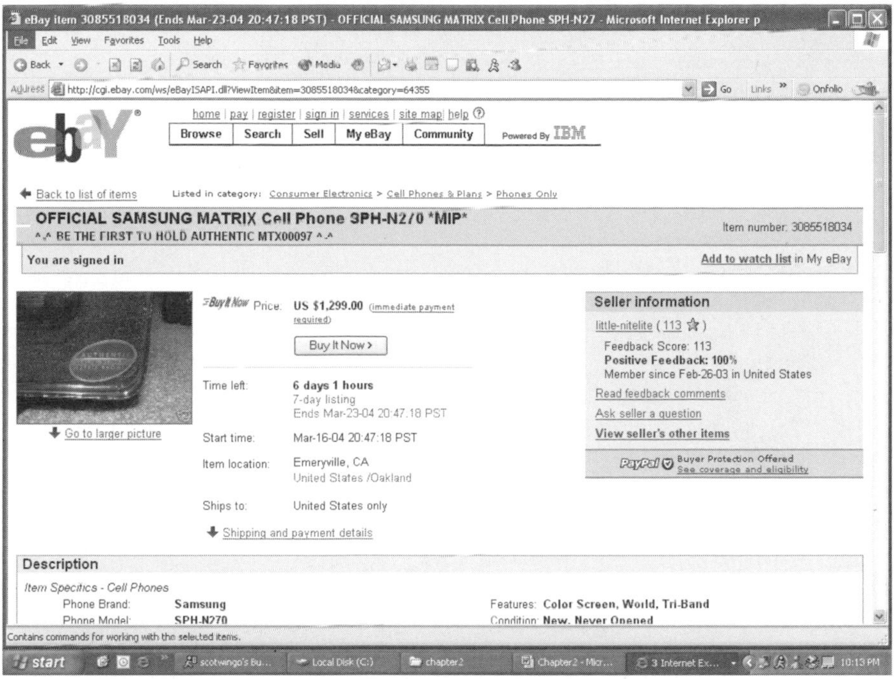

FIGURE 2.1 An immediate payment auction listing with BIN

Average Sales Price

Another important vital sign for your eBay business is your *average sales price,* or ASP. ASP is calculated by dividing GMS for a period of time by the number of items sold during that period. For example, SellerX's GMS for June is $10,000. SellerX sold 475 items during this period. So SellerX's ASP is $21.05 ($10,000 ÷ 475).

ASP can also be narrowed to consider a certain item, or SKU (short for stock keeping unit). In this case, we use the term *SKU ASP.* For example, let's say SellerX has two items, SKU1 and SKU2. During June, SellerX sells 500 units of SKU1, for $5,000. Also, during June, SellerX sells 50 units of SKU2, for $1,000.

SKU—stock keeping unit—is a term frequently used by off-line retailers to designate a unique item of inventory. The key to SKUs is that they are unique items. For example, let's say you have three sweaters:

1. Red XL

2. Blue L

3. Red XL

There are only two sweater SKUs: Red XL (quantity 2) and Blue L (quantity 1).

SKU1 has an SKU ASP of $10 ($5,000 ÷ 500) and SKU2 has a SKU ASP of $20 ($1,000 ÷ 50).

ASP is an important measure, because by monitoring your ASP over time, you can get a feeling for how your products are doing in the marketplace (assuming your inventory mix is relatively constant over the periods being measured). SKU ASP will help you determine the margin for a particular SKU over a period of time.

Average Order Value and Items per Order

Average order value, or AOV, applies if you are able to consolidate multiple items into a single order on eBay. If you consolidate, then AOV provides a way to measure any increases or decreases in the value of each order (with potentially multiple items) or the rate of consolidation. AOV is calculated by dividing the GMS over a period of time by the number of orders over the same time frame. Another interesting measurement when you are able to consolidate orders is the ratio of *items per order* (IPO).

For example, if SellerX has $4,000 in GMS for May and 100 orders for 175 items, his AOV is $40 ($4,000 ÷ 100) and the IPO is 1.75 (175 ÷ 100).

AOV and IPO are very useful for measuring the rate at which buyers are consolidating items and buying more than one item from you on average. Imagine if you could sell twice as much to each buyer: that would double your business without a huge increase in effort. Also, for items in the $1–$50 range, buyers enjoy consolidation because it allows them to get more for their shipping fees. Later you will see how you can charge consolidated shipping rates and then measure your AOV/IPO to see what impact that has on your eBay business.

Conversion Rate

This metric is the most discussed vital sign of an eBay business. Nearly every seller calculates it differently and calls it by a different name. *Sell through, success rate, closure rate, winner rate,* and *bidder rate* are just a few of the terms used. In this book, we call it *conversion rate* (CR).

We define CR as the number of *items* sold divided by the number of *items* posted or listed over a time frame:

Conversion rate (%) = Number of *items* sold ÷ Number of *items* listed

Note that items sold and listed have to be over the same exact time frame. Note also that we highlight items here so that when using multi-quantity auction listings or multi-quantity fixed-price listings, you count each *item*, not each *listing*.

Also, we recommend using the same definition of CR for eBay Stores but separating that rate from your other eBay business. So you have two conversion rates to track: your eBay conversion rate and your eBay Stores conversion rate.

Some confusion about CR results from relists. On eBay, when an item does not sell the first time, you can relist the item; if it sells the second time, you receive a credit for the relist.

In our experience, you should definitely use relists as a way to lower eBay fees. However, when calculating CR, since choosing to relist an item is the same business decision as posting a new item, relists should be counted as new items—and you can incur another listing fee if the item does not sell.

As with GMS, NPBs impact conversion rates as well. Thus, you have gross CR (without NPBs) and net CR (with NPBs). If your NPB rate is relatively low (less than 2%), then you can track just one of these vitals. If your NPB rate is higher, though, you should track both sets of CRs.

EXAMPLE 1

In July, SellerX lists 1,000 items, and 425 of them sell successfully. SellerX has a CR of 42.5% (425 ÷ 1,000).

EXAMPLE 2

In July, SellerX lists 10 Dutch auctions, each with a quantity of 10. SellerX sells 42 items out of the 100 items in the 10 listings. SellerX has a CR of 42% (42 ÷ 100).

EXAMPLE 3

In August, SellerX lists 1,000 items, and 425 close with a winning bidder. SellerX unfortunately experiences 40 NPBs. SellerX's gross CR is 42.5%, and his net CR is 38.5%.

EXAMPLE 4

In September, SellerX lists 2,000 items on eBay, of which 1,000 sell. SellerX also lists 4,000 items in an eBay Store, of which 100 sell. SellerX has an eBay CR of 50% (1,000 ÷ 2,000) and an eBay Store CR of 2.5% (100 ÷ 4,000).

Margin

Ultimately, all businesses exist to generate profits, and there is no better measurement of success than *margin* (sometimes called, somewhat confusingly, net income).

Margin is simply the profit your eBay business makes over a period of time, taking all costs into consideration (such as eBay fees, PayPal fees, costs of goods, labor, shipping and handling, rent, and so on).

In addition to margin, another useful metric is your margin as a percentage of GMS. For example, if SellerX has a GMS of $10,000 and makes $1,000 in margin a month, then SellerX's margin percentage is 10%.

Later in this chapter, we provide a simple format for an eBay business income statement, which you can use to calculate your absolute and percentage margin.

KNOW YOUR CRITICAL EBAY VITALS!

This brings us to our first key eBay strategy: Know Your Vitals. A great eBay business operator knows her GMS, ASP, and CR off the top of her head for the week, month, quarter, and year. Here are some of the powerful benefits you will get from knowing your eBay vitals.

Noticing Positive and Negative Trends in Your Business

If you know and monitor your vitals on a weekly, if not daily, basis, you will catch any positive or negative trends in your business. For example, we recently had one seller whose ASP and CR took steep increases in the middle of the month. We were able to trace this change to an update in the look and feel of the seller's About Me page and to listings that we had made the previous week. Much to our surprise, a simple merchandising change had increased both of these metrics substantially. After noticing this, we continued to tweak the merchandising for even more benefit.

Conversely, we frequently see sudden decreases in ASP and CR, which are important to catch immediately and investigate; they can indicate a number of potential problems. For example, we recently had a digital camera seller experience a sharp CR decrease. Upon further investigation, we discovered another seller was offering largely the same items but at prices 5 to 10% lower than our seller's prices. We were able to vary the inventory and lower some prices to counter this competitive situation rapidly—rather than noticing it weeks or even months later.

Note that a decrease in one of your eBay vitals isn't necessarily a bad thing. It's better to take a more holistic approach to your eBay business. For example, your ASP may drop, but your overall margin can go up. Also, your CR and GMS can decrease, but absolute margin may increase. The key is to establish goals for your business and determine what vital changes are required to achieve those goals.

Experiments and Changes to Your Vitals

Knowing your vitals will also allow you to experiment—and then to see what effect the experiments have on your vitals. For example, we had a cell phone seller who tried selling accessories. Within 30 days, the accessories had:

- Increased GMS by 10%

- Decreased ASP by 25%

- Decreased CR by 10%

- Increased AOV by 10%

- Increased IPO by 30%

- Increased margin by 15%

The point is, if we had focused only on CR and ASP, this experiment would have looked like a complete failure. This seller's goal was to increase margin, and he was able to do that by putting accessories—with much higher margins than cell phones—into the mix.

How eBay Vitals Are Interrelated

Once you know and can track your critical vitals, you will see how they interact with your business. For example, in almost every eBay business, a decrease in conversion rates—assuming all other vitals are the same—means a substantial decrease in margin, because eBay fees increase when conversion rates decrease.

Generally, an increase in ASP will have positive implications for GMS and margin, because you are doing the same amount of work with higher results. The same can also be said of AOV and IPO: those two metrics will dramatically move the needle on GMS and margin, usually positively, unless some low-margin products are being added onto orders.

The Relative Health of Your eBay Business

Once you know your eBay vital stats, you can compare them to the eBay average and to those of other sellers you may know. At the time of this writing and based on public information and privately calculated information, the averages for eBay are the following:

- **GMS.** This metric varies widely among sellers. We calculate that the average GMS for sellers is around $500 per month. This average is deceptive, because there are different "tiers" of sellers. The lower tier, which includes individuals and hobbyists, is the largest in terms of numbers, but they do a relatively small amount of GMS.

- **ASP.** The ASP across all of eBay is $50. Note that this varies per category. For example, in computers, the ASP is in the $500–$800 range, and in CDs the ASP is in the $5–$8 range.

- **CR.** The average conversion rate on eBay is 45–50% and varies by category. The CD and DVD categories have lower CRs, and the electronics category has one of the highest CRs.

- **Margin, AOV, and IPO.** These eBay vitals are not known for most sellers. In fact, most sellers cannot or do not combine orders, so AOVs and IPOs are probably very low across all of eBay.

What-If Scenarios

Knowing your eBay vitals lets you do some planning and analysis of what-if scenarios. For example, you can say:

"What if I increase my listings by 10%?" Then you can assume your CR will decrease some, your ASP may decrease some, and your GMS and margin will increase or decrease, based on the impact to CR and ASP. Once you model these out, you can take the what-if action (listing more items, in this example) and see how GMS, CR, ASP, and margin end up compared to your planned values.

Once you have gone through this exercise for about six months, your feel for your eBay business model will be like driving a car. You'll know when to hit the brakes, when to clutch, and when to hit the gas!

USE YOUR CURRENT VITALS TO SEE WHAT IT WOULD TAKE TO BE A MILLION-DOLLAR EBAY BUSINESS

Here's a fun example you can go through now to see what it would be like for you to run a million-dollar-a-year eBay business. If you already have a million-dollar-a-year eBay business, then your goal can be to double your business.

Let's assume we have an eBay business with these vitals:

- **GMS**: $20,000 per month

- **ASP**: $60

- **CR**: 50%

- **Margin**: 7%

Given these metrics, we're also able to determine that this seller:

1. Sells 333 items per month ($20,000 ÷ $60).

2. Lists or posts 666 items per month (listings = transactions ÷ CR, or 333 ÷ 0.50).

For this seller to be a million-dollar-a-year seller, he needs to take his GMS from $20,000 to $85,000 per month. Thus, assuming a constant CR and ASP, he would need to:

1. Sell 1,416 items per month ($85,000 ÷ $60). Note that this implies he will need to buy and inventory these items before posting.

2. Ship 47 items a day.

3. List or post 2,833 items per month.

4. List 95 items a day.

Go through this exercise for your business, and you will then be able to ask yourself what you need to do if you want to reach this level of activity. How many people would you need? Do you have software and other infrastructure that can handle the volume? How would you ship this much? Where would you store 1,416 items a month?

Noncritical Vitals

In addition to the critical eBay business vital metrics, a couple of noncritical measurements can allow you to fine-tune your eBay business.

Take Rate

When you start looking into your margin, the *take rate* (TR) is an important statistic to measure. Take rate is calculated by simply dividing your eBay fees by your GMS to get a percentage.

For example, SellerX sells $20,000 a month and has a monthly eBay bill of $1,400. Therefore, SellerX's TR is 7% ($1,400 ÷ $20,000). Note that TR does not count PayPal fees.

The average TR for all of eBay is in the range of 7 to 8%. This may seem high given that final value fees start at 5.25% and go down, but look at an example. SellerX has the following statistics:

- **A 50% conversion rate and an ASP of $50**

- **A starting auction price of $25**

- **A policy of using BIN ($0.05)**

- **eBay picture hosting ($0.15)**

- **$20,000 a month in sales**

Based on these data points, we can calculate the following:

- **400 items ($20,000 ÷ 50) are sold a month.**

- **800 items are posted a month.**

- **Listing fees per item are $0.05 (BIN) + $0.15 (pics) + $0.60 (insertion fee) = $0.80.**

- **Final value fees per $50 item sold are $1.31 + $0.68 = $1.99.**

- **Total fees are ($0.80 × 800) + ($1.99 × 400) = $640 + $796 = $1,436.**

- **$1,436 ÷ $20,000 = 7.18% TR**

The preceding example illustrates that given eBay's averages, you can plan for your TR to be in the 7% to 8% range. TR illustrates the importance of knowing and tracking your eBay vitals, because they drive your TR. For example, if your ASP is less than $50 and your conversion rate decreases, your eBay fees as a percentage of GMS skyrocket.

Let's take two extreme examples to illustrate this point and show how ASP and CR work in concert to drive TR.

EXAMPLE 1

SellerA sells VHS tapes and has the following eBay vitals:

- **$20,000 per month GMS**
- **$8 ASP**
- **All items start at $0.99**
- **10% conversion rate**

EXAMPLE 2

SellerB sells laptops and has the following eBay vitals:

- **$20,000 per month GMS**
- **$350 ASP**
- **All items start at $9.99**
- **90% conversion rate**

The TR for Example 1 is this:

- **SellerA sells 2,500 items ($20,000 ÷ 8) per month.**
- **SellerA lists 25,000 items (2,500 ÷ 0.10) per month.**
- **Listing fee per item: $0.20 (assuming pictures and BIN) + $0.30 = $0.50 per item listed.**
- **FVF per item: (5.25% × $8) = $0.42 per item sold.**
- **SellerA's fees are ($0.50 × 25,000) + ($0.42 × 2,500) = $12,500 + $1,050 = $13,550.**
- **SellerA's TR is a massive 67.8%!! ($13,550 ÷ $20,000)**

The TR for Example 2 is this:

- **SellerB sells 57 items ($20,000 ÷ 350) per month.**

- **SellerB lists 63 items (57 ÷ 0.90) per month.**

- **Listing fee per item: $0.20 (assuming pictures and BIN) + $0.35 = $0.55 per item listed.**

- **FVF fee per item: $1.31 + (2.75% × $325) = $10.24 per item sold.**

- **SellerB's fees are ($0.55 × 63) + ($10.24 × 57) = $34.65 + $583.68 = $618.33.**

- **SellerB's TR is a petite 3.1%!! ($618.33 ÷ $20,000)**

These examples illustrate the broad spectrum of TR based on ASP and CR (holding all other things constant). Believe it or not, there are sellers like SellerA whose listing fees alone are more than 20% of their GMS. These are clearly broken business models, and the businesses are on the brink of extinction—if they aren't already out of business.

To help you find where your business is in the spectrum and what it would look like if you vary ASP or conversion rate or both, Table 2.2 shows a range of data points.

Table 2.2 illustrates the eBay fees as a percentage of sales for a variety of CR and ASP options, given that all else stays the same. In this example, all items were listed for $0.99 with no reserve and no optional fees such as BIN, image hosting, or promotion. Note that such extra insertion fees have the largest impact on the $5 to $40 ASPs, because they represent a very low percentage of higher ASPs.

By now you are hopefully not too shocked about where your TR is today and where it could or should be. Regardless of your current TR, the goal of the strategic framework presented next is to help you drive those vitals in the

			CR				
ASP	**20%**	**30%**	**40%**	**50%**	**60%**	**70%**	**100%**
10	20.25%	15.25%	12.75%	11.25%	10.25%	9.54%	8.25%
20	19.00%	14.42%	12.13%	10.75%	9.83%	9.18%	8.00%
40	18.06%	13.48%	11.19%	9.81%	8.89%	8.24%	7.06%
80	17.28%	12.70%	10.41%	9.03%	8.11%	7.46%	6.28%
100	14.37%	10.70%	8.87%	7.77%	7.04%	6.51%	5.57%
200	11.31%	8.56%	7.19%	6.36%	5.81%	5.42%	4.71%
1000	4.46%	3.91%	3.64%	3.47%	3.36%	3.28%	3.14%

TABLE 2.2 eBay fees take rate across a variety of ASPs and CRs

right direction, which will have the corresponding benefit of lowering your TR and increasing your margin.

BIN Rate

BIN rate is the percentage of items you sell via fixed price. For this calculation, we include BIN auction-style listings and fixed-price listings, but not store listings.

For example, in June, SellerX sold 1,000 items, 257 of which were BIN/fixed price. SellerX has a 25.7% BIN rate.

Note that the average BIN rate across eBay is about 25%, and we advocate moving this to the 40–60% range, if possible.

Shipping and Handling Margin

About a third of sellers use shipping and handling (S+H) as a source of profits. Another third break even, and another third actually lose money when they factor all costs into the equation. We define *S+H margin* as the difference between what you charge for shipping and handling and what it costs you. S+H costs include:

- Postage
- Boxing materials
- Packing materials
- Insurance (if any)
- Any extra shipping costs incurred

N O T E

Taxes are a pass-through cost and are not part of shipping and handling.

For example, over the course of a month, SellerX receives $2,450 in S+H charges. SellerX's costs over that period are $2,000. So, SellerX had a S+H margin of $450, or 18%.

What about Feedback?!?

You may be wondering why feedback isn't a key eBay vital sign. Although feedback is an important aspect of your eBay business, once it's more than 100 or so, we have found that its value isn't that critical to your success. Feedback is more indicative of your customer service (which is important) and buyer fraud than your actual sales. For example, which of these sellers do you think does more GMS and makes more margin:

- returnbuy (43451 ★) me (96.8% positive)
- mobilepc (3040 ★) Power Seller me (98.2% positive)

Using the feedback rating (43451 for returnbuy and 3040 for mobilepc), it would appear that returnbuy is by far the superior seller (by a factor of 10). However, returnbuy hasn't sold anything since 2003, and mobilepc is a top eBay seller by GMS.

continued

continued

GMS is not equal to feedback, and feedback is not necessarily an indicator of GMS.

Strong feedback can have an impact on GMS (actually raising the ASP compared to competitors with lower feedback), but great feedback on eBay is so common that we have found buyers lump sellers into one of two categories: great feedback or bad feedback. The bad feedback category is for those with a negative feedback rating, or a positive one lower than 95%—or those with a large number of recent negatives.

Once a buyer puts you in the "good seller" category, there are many other ways you can increase your ASP that are more effective than getting your feedback from 1,000 to 10,000. We will cover these in detail later as part of the strategic framework.

Attach Rate and Attach ASP

If you are able to up-sell in your checkout system, two metrics that are important to track are the rate at which people up-sell—called the *attach rate*—and the ASP of the items up-sold, or the *attach ASP*.

For example, SellerX sells 500 items a month and up-sells 20 items a month for an additional $1,100 in GMS. SellerX's attach rate is 4% (20 ÷ 500), and the attach ASP is $55 ($1,100 ÷ 20).

A Tale of Two Documents

To drive your eBay business forward, you will need two basic accounting documents: an income statement (sometimes called a profit-and-loss statement, or P+L) and a balance sheet. In the next two sections, we present a simplified income statement and a balance sheet that we have found useful for eBay businesses. Note that if you are using software such as QuickBooks or Peachtree, you should be able to customize the reports in those packages to line up with the formats presented here.

Your eBay Business Income Statement

The income statement is useful to show all of your incomes, your costs, and your margin over a given time frame. A sample income statement follows, with descriptions in parentheses.

```
                    INCOME STATEMENT

                      GMS
                  +   S+H Income
                  −   Cost of Goods Sold (COGS)
                  −   S+H Cost
GROSS MARGIN      _____
PERCENTAGE
OF INCOME         _____


               OTHER EXPENSES

                  −   eBay Fees
                  −   Payment Processing Fees
                  −   Labor and Health Insurance
                  −   Rent
                  −   Insurance
                  −   Other Costs
NET MARGIN        _____
PERCENTAGE
OF INCOME         _____
```

Here is an example of a simple, real-life eBay business income statement.

INCOME STATEMENT FOR 1/1/04–2/1/04

	$25,000	GMS
+	$ 4,000	S+H Income
−	$18,000	Cost of Goods Sold (COGS)
−	$ 3,750	S+H Cost
GROSS MARGIN	$ 7,250	
PERCENTAGE OF INCOME	25% ($7.250 ÷ $29,000)	

OTHER EXPENSES

−	$1,750	eBay Fees
−	$ 550	Payment Processing Fees
−	$1,000	Labor and Health Insurance
−	$ 750	Rent
−	$ 600	Property Insurance
−	$ 450	Other Costs
NET MARGIN	$2,150	
MARGIN PERCENTAGE	7.41% ($2,150 ÷ $29,000)	

As you can see, this income statement makes it easy to calculate many of your eBay vital statistics, such as GMS, margin, S+H margin, and so on. It also gives you two important percentages you should watch and work to improve: *gross margin* and *net margin*. In this example, a gross margin of 25% and a net margin of 7.41% are good. To increase gross margin, you essentially need to sell your products for more or increase your margin rate on S+H, or both. To increase your net margin, you need to decrease your non-product costs, such as eBay fees, payment fees, and others.

Throughout the rest of the book, we highlight several ways to increase your net margin and gross margin.

Your eBay Business Balance Sheet

A balance sheet is a way of showing both the assets and the liabilities of your business. As the name suggests, your balance sheet should "balance," or add up. An income statement covers a *given period of time*; a balance sheet pertains to a *given date in time*.

BALANCE SHEET FOR JULY 1, 2004

ASSETS

+ Cash

+ Inventory

+ Other Assets

LIABILITIES

− Debt

− Accounts Payable

NET ASSETS _____

Following is an example of a balance sheet from a real eBay business.

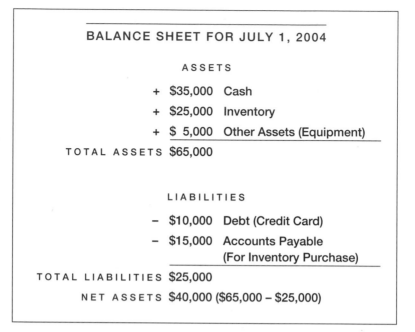

BALANCE SHEET FOR JULY 1, 2004

ASSETS

+ $35,000 Cash
+ $25,000 Inventory
+ $ 5,000 Other Assets (Equipment)

TOTAL ASSETS $65,000

LIABILITIES

− $10,000 Debt (Credit Card)
− $15,000 Accounts Payable
           (For Inventory Purchase)

TOTAL LIABILITIES $25,000
NET ASSETS $40,000 ($65,000 − $25,000)

Now that you have your eBay vital statistics, a basic income statement, and a balance sheet, you possess the foundation for taking your business to the next level. In Chapter 3, we introduce the strategic framework: the Five P's.

Chapter 2 Summary

Gross merchandise sales (GMS) — The volume of your sales on eBay.

Non-paying bidder rate (NPB rate) — The rate at which your items are left unpaid by non-paying bidders. Formula: $NPB ÷ $GMS = NPB rate.

Average sales price (ASP) — The average sales price over a period of time. Formula: GMS ÷ number of sales = ASP.

Stock keeping unit (SKU) — An individual, unique inventory item.

Average order value (AOV) — The average value of orders, a metric that is useful if you are consolidating orders (that is, selling more than one item per order). Formula: GMS ÷ number of orders = AOV.

Items per order (IPO) — The number of items per order, another measurement that is useful if you are consolidating orders. Formula: number of items ÷ number of orders = IPO.

Conversion rate (CR) — The pace at which your listed items are selling, expressed as a percentage. Formula: number of items listed ÷ number of items sold = CR.

Margin — The ultimate cash generated by your business, sometimes called net income, "the bottom line," or profit.

Take rate (TR) — The amount, expressed in a percentage, of your GMS that goes toward eBay fees. Formula: eBay fees ÷ GMS = TR.

BIN rate — The percentage of items sold that are attributable to the BIN and fixed-price formats. Formula: BIN or FP items sold ÷ total items sold = BIN rate.

S+H margin — The margin (or loss) made on shipping and handling, expressed as both an absolute value and a percentage.

Attach rate — If your checkout supports up-selling, the rate at which customers are up-sold, or at which they attach items to the original order. Formula: items up-sold per month ÷ total items sold = attach rate.

Attach ASP — The average selling price of items that are attached as a secondary item onto a primary purchase. Formula: up-sold GMS ÷ number of up-sold items = attach ASP.

Chapter 2 Summary

The goal of this chapter is to build a foundation of the business concepts you need to know well in order to drive your business forward. The key concepts are:

eBay listings. We reviewed the three types of eBay listings: auction-style, fixed price, and eBay Store.

eBay fees. We explained the eBay fee structure, which every seller should know by heart, because it is a significant cost for most sellers that should be tracked via TR.

eBay vital signs. Just as a doctor reviews your vital signs to determine your health, you should monitor and review your eBay vital signs, as just reiterated in the "New Terminology" section.

Strategy 1. This chapter introduced the first strategy: Know Your Vital Signs. Basically, this strategy says that once you know your eBay vitals, you can experiment, run what-if scenarios, and learn how the eBay vitals for your eBay business are related. For example, what would happen to your eBay vitals if you were to list 15% more this month?

Feedback. Feedback is an important part of eBay and a great measure of how you are doing with customer service, but it's not generally related to the health of your business or how much one seller is selling versus another.

Income statement. If you don't already have an income statement, or if you would like to improve what you have, you can use the basic eBay business income statement we provided. This income statement highlights your GMS, gross margin, and net margin—three key indicators of how any retail business is doing.

Balance sheet. Finally, we introduced an eBay business balance sheet to help you keep track of your assets, liabilities, and (hopefully) net assets.

Chapter 2 Summary

http://pages.ebay.com/help/sell/ formats.html

A description of eBay listing types

http://pages.ebay.com/help/sell/ fees.html

An overview of eBay fees

http://www.intuit.com

The makers of Quicken and QuickBooks, a popular accounting package used by eBay businesses

http://www.peachtree.com

The home of Peachtree Accounting, another popular accounting package

EXERCISES

1. Calculate your eBay vitals in a notebook or a spreadsheet. Which ones are most important to your business? Which ones do you think you can improve? Which ones do you think will be hardest to change?

2. Calculate what it would take for you to have a million-dollar-a-year eBay business. (If you're already there, how can you double your business?)

eBay

Introducing the "Five P's": The Strategic eBay Framework

The strategic eBay framework, a.k.a. the Five P's

When working to scale your eBay business, it is very easy to spend all your time in the "weeds," or details, of running your business. Instead of thinking about the big picture, the average eBay businessperson spends more time worrying about fraud, shipping, eBay fees, listing schedules, and so on. Although these aspects of an eBay business are important, if you spend all of your time on the details, you'll neglect the bigger picture. As a result, the business "treads water" instead of growing.

As an eBay business owner, even if you have time to think about the big picture, you have an overwhelming number of strategic decisions to make:

- **What product should I source?**

- **How can I best promote my products?**

- **How should I price my items?**

- **How much of a certain SKU should I buy (and how much can I sell in a certain amount of time)?**

- **What eBay strategy should I use for each item I have to sell?**

- **In what categories should I sell?**

- **How do all of these decisions affect my eBay vitals and the corresponding health of my business?**

Given the overwhelming nature of these questions, we have found that most eBay sellers find a comfort zone and stay there. In other words, they find a product source that works for them in a specific category, find a strategy that works, and stick to it. Once all of the strategic questions are "answered," they stay fixed. The only thing most sellers do to scale their business is more of the same, and they drive sales only by buying more.

Depending on the business's eBay vitals, this "single-focus" strategy works for sellers who earn as much as $20,000 to $100,000 per month, but it is very risky. For example, if a new competitor enters the field and you are focused solely on something like digital camera lenses, that competitor can rapidly cause your business to fall apart, because you have put all your eggs in one basket.

To help sellers focus on the strategic big picture of their eBay business—and to do so efficiently—we have developed the Five P's strategic framework. This framework gives you an important and proven tool to help you make strategic decisions. We recommend all eBay businesspeople spend at least 20% of their time (that's about one day a week) and if possible as much as 50% of their time focusing on their eBay business strategy by using the strategic framework.

The Five P's

To help you remember the framework, we have given it a name that's easy to remember (there's a *P* for each finger) and a visual representation that summarizes the framework. You can find the diagram at the beginning of this chapter and on the inside cover of the book. Here are the five components of the strategic framework:

1. **Product. One of the most important strategic decisions you make in an eBay business is what product you source and ultimately sell. Focusing on this *P* will help you think about not only sourcing product, but also some other strategic ways you can leverage the product you buy to dramatically increase your eBay sales. For example, have you thought about also sourcing add-ons to your core products as a way to boost sales and margin?**

2. **Price.** How much should you pay for products? For how much should you try to sell them? What is the best eBay strategy to obtain the maximum price for your goods? Should you start everything at $1.00 with no reserve and see what happens or use BIN?

3. **Promotion.** Can promotion increase your eBay results? If so, what are the best promotions? Which ones are included with your eBay listing fees and for which ones must you pay extra? If you pay extra, what is the best return on your investment?

4. **Placement.** Another important strategic decision is where to place products. You can make this decision after you have sourced product, or you may think about it when you source product. If you're selling on eBay only, *placement* refers to the category in which you will sell. For example, should you put a pair of sneakers in apparel or sporting goods? If you have your own e-commerce system (which we highly recommend—see Chapter 7) or an eBay Store, or if you sell on another auction site, you must decide on which of these channels to place your product or on which one(s) to source product to sell.

5. **Performance.** In Chapter 2, we introduced several eBay vital signs that are a great way to measure your business. As you make strategic decisions guided by the first four *P's*, the last *P*—performance—will let you see in real time how those decisions are affecting the vitals of your business. Like the dashboard in your car, you can create a simple control center that will help you understand how fast your business is growing and keep track of other critical eBay statistics that determine the health of your business.

As the diagram of the Five P's shows, each *P* feeds into the next. As you will see, although we can consider each separately, we also have to think of how they interact. In other words, when you are sourcing some *product,* you should already have thought about how that product could improve your *performance,* as well as how you plan to *price* it, *promote* it, and the product's potential *placement.*

Your product, pricing, promotion, and placement decisions are what drive your eBay business's performance. As the diagram shows, performance is at the core of the framework, because measuring the impact of the other parts of the framework will help you drive your business as fast as possible.

To remember the Five P's, you should try reciting them ten times every day until you have them committed to memory. Say it with me: "Product. Price. Promotion. Placement. Performance." Again: "Product. Price. Promotion. Placement. Performance."

How to Use the Five P's

At this point you may be thinking: "This Five P's thing is interesting, but how can I use it in my everyday business?" That's a good question. The Five P's are a strategic business framework, and like the framework of a building, until you start to use the framework, it really has no value.

Each of the following chapters takes one of the *P's* of the framework and provides some real-world concepts you can use for that part of the framework. Each also includes a case study for each of the *P's.* Finally, a case study for the complete Five P's framework is presented in Chapter 9, so you can see how a real eBay business has leveraged the framework for success.

2 SET YOUR STRATEGIC GOALS

To get the most out of the Five P's framework, you must first set strategic goals for your eBay business. By *strategic,* we mean "involving the big picture." For example, "I want to ship packages in half the time I do today" is not a strategic goal; it is a tactical goal. However, "I want to expand into an entirely new category by the end of the year" is a strategic goal.

What should your goal be? The beauty of eBay is there is virtually no limit to how large your business can be, so you can dream big. Do you want a million-dollar eBay business? Do you want to double or triple your current business? Or do you want to keep your GMS about the same and really focus on the bottom-line margin?

Whatever your goal, you should include some detailed time frames and eBay vital statistics. For example, simply saying "I want to increase my sales!" is vague, and it doesn't answer some important questions: When? What about margin? Increase from what to what? A better goal would be this:

> A year from now, I want my eBay business GMS to triple from $10,000 per month to $30,000 per month. Additionally, I would like to maintain margin and use this opportunity to expand into one or two new categories. Finally, I would like to increase my ASP and improve CR.

This type of strategic goal is much easier to start thinking about and to plan for, because of the specific time frame and the very focused eBay vital targets.

Here's how. Let's take this example one step further, by breaking it into four quarterly milestones:

- Q1—Increase GMS from $10,000 to $15,000 per month

- Q2—Increase GMS from $15,000 to $20,000 per month

- Q3—Increase GMS from $20,000 to $25,000 per month

- Q4—Increase GMS from $25,000 to $30,000 per month

From here, you can even take things down to the day and month. For example, in Q1, the increase of $5,000 from $10,000 to $15,000 would be:

- Month 1: Increase GMS from $10,000 to $11,500

- Month 2: Increase GMS from $11,500 to $13,000

- Month 3: Increase GMS from $13,000 to $15,000

For Month 1, you would start the month at $333 per day in sales ($10,000 ÷ 30) and end at $383 per day in sales ($11,500 ÷ 30).

If you know your eBay vital statistics such as your ASP and CR, you can even start looking at how many items you will need to post and sell to get to the daily / weekly / quarterly and annual goals.

In fact, to help you set your goals and plan for them, we've made a spreadsheet available at the book's Web site: http://ebaystrategies.blogs.com. The spreadsheet will allow you to plug in your current eBay vitals and your goal eBay vitals. The spreadsheet will then automatically calculate a one-year plan with detail down to the quarter, month, and day. See the sample in Figure 3.1.

The goals in the spreadsheet are just that: goals. Most likely, the goals you have set for your eBay business will not be achievable by maintaining the status quo and just "doing more of the same." Even if that were possible, it is

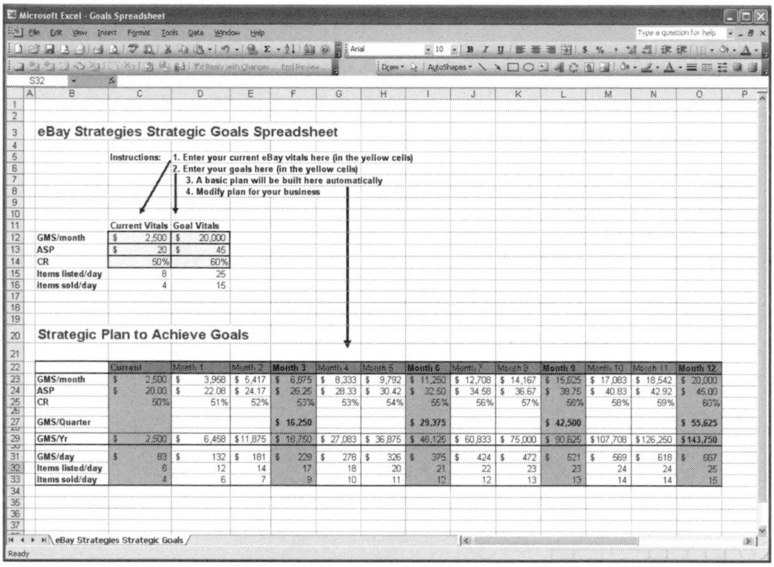

FIGURE 3.1   The eBay goals spreadsheet

not advisable, because on the way to achieving your goals, you need to be careful to diversify your business and grow solidly. Otherwise, you might fall into one of the many pitfalls that have caused very large eBay businesses to flame out. (See Chapter 1 for more on flameouts.)

Also realize right now that achieving your goals will take a great deal of work, experimentation, and perseverance: you may not always move forward one step at a time. Sometimes to grow your eBay business, you may need to take one step back to get two steps forward. For example, if you want to expand into new categories, that process can take a month or two to try out one, probably two or three new categories, before you find the right category for your business. It's important to stick to it and keep coming back to the Five P's—they will act as your guiding light to success.

Your goal should be one that you fundamentally believe is achievable and to which you are willing to totally dedicate yourself and your team (if you have one). One of my favorite quotes is "Try not. Do, or do not. There is no try." (Yoda, from *Star Wars: The Empire Strikes Back*)

What's the point of setting these goals if you're not going to achieve them? The "goals" spreadsheet will let you do a sanity check. Once you feel comfortable with the goals, you *will* be able to use the Five P's to achieve them. (Notice that we didn't say "try"!!)

In conclusion, the Five P's strategic framework is not a silver bullet. It does not magically improve your business. You must set clear strategic goals and consider how each *P* will help you achieve the goals you have set.

Chapter 3 Summary

Five P's—An easy-to-remember mnemonic for the eBay business strategic framework

KEY CONCEPTS

In this chapter, we introduced the Five P's strategic framework, whose goal is to help sellers focus on the forest instead of the trees. It is strongly recommended that sellers spend 20 to 50% of their time considering the Five P's of their business, rather than dealing with tactical, day-to-day issues. The Five P's are:

- **Product.** Everything to do with the product that you source and sell, including its age, margin, category, add-ons, and more.

- **Price.** How you price your products for sale and all of the strategies associated with achieving that price.

- **Promotion.** How you promote your products using "free" and "paid" promotional options at your disposal.

- **Placement.** Where you choose to sell your product. In addition to the online venue, this can include the particular eBay category.

- **Performance.** As the Five P's figure illustrates, performance is the core of the Five P's strategy. Every decision made in terms of product, price, promotion, and placement must be tracked to measure its effectiveness. The decisions that are effective can be enhanced, and those that do not achieve the desired goals can be dialed back.

The Five P's will make it much easier to achieve your strategic goals, but you can't put the cart in front of the horse. Before moving on to the next chapter, you need to establish your strategic goals and use the provided "goals"

Chapter 3 Summary

spreadsheet to generate a basic map that shows your goals and the corresponding eBay vitals needed to achieve those goals.

EXERCISES

1. What are the Five P's? Can you recite them without looking at the book? Try writing them down on a piece of paper from memory exactly one hour from now, or before you go to bed tonight.

2. For the next day, think about every decision you make regarding your business and try to place each decision into one of the P's. If it doesn't fit, is your decision about "trees" (that is, a tactical one) or about "the forest" (a strategic one)?

3. Try to sketch the Five P's diagram from memory.

4. Keep a short journal (or a log on your computer) of decisions you make that fall into the Five P's. After at least seven days, calculate the percentage of your time spent on strategic versus tactical tasks.

5. **Important**: Before moving forward in this book, write down specific goals (concerning a time frame and your eBay vitals) for your eBay business. For example: "In the next six months, my GMS will increase 25% and I will increase my ASP and improve my CR while keeping my margin percentage the same as it is today."

eBay

Product

The first P in the strategic eBay framework: product

The first *P* of the Five P's strategic framework we will explore is *product*. Without product, you would obviously not have an eBay business. In fact, product usually determines the focus of your eBay business, how you market the business, and many other aspects of your strategy. In this chapter, we discuss all aspects of product, ranging from sourcing to product mix and how deep and wide you should be on product. Although sourcing product is one of the most important tasks you perform in your eBay business, we cover it last because it's essential to set your product strategy before you start sourcing product. Before we go into those details, let's explore the concept of a product's life cycle.

The Product Life Cycle

As a buyer or consumer of various products, you have probably noticed that products go through a life cycle. As a seller, you need to be more aware of the product life cycle, because it will influence the types of products you source and sell via your eBay business.

Figure 4.1 shows the product life cycle as most large manufacturers and retailers view it. The curve in Figure 4.1 shows the typical sales volume for a product over its life cycle, "from the cradle to the grave." Note that this is the curve for almost all categories of consumer-oriented products. The exception to the curve is collectibles, which frequently sell more at the end of their life cycle than at the beginning. For example, a CD for a soundtrack may have been a flop when it was first introduced, but then, two years later, the film attains cult status and the soundtrack sells for ten times more than its release value. Remember that collectibles can happen in all categories, not just the traditional ones such as Beanie Babies. For example, some

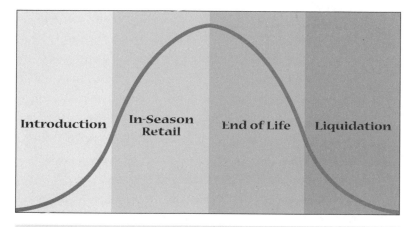

FIGURE 4.1 The four phases of the product life cycle

automobiles become collectibles; video games can attract collectors; and even items considered commodities, such as calculators, can become collectible.

As shown in Figure 4.1, the four phases of the product life cycle are:

■ **Phase 1—Introduction.** Also known as product launch, this phase occurs when the product is released to the market and it is very new in consumers' minds. At this phase of the life cycle for hot and exciting products, the supply of products can be a good bit behind the demand for them. This situation indicates a healthy product life cycle that can last from one to three years. Or if the product is a flop, the supply will actually be greater than demand, which indicates an unhealthy life cycle and usually results in a six- to twelve-month cycle or less.

For example, at the time of this writing, Apple had recently released the iPod Mini, an MP3 player that has been sold out for the three months since its introduction. Conversely, a consumer electronics company released a $1,000 kitchen appliance for surfing the Web that was a flop and ended up in the discount bin two months after its release.

■ **Phase 2—In-season retail.** When you go to your local retail establishment, the bulk of what is for sale is in-season retail. The latest and greatest digital camera, cars, books, televisions, sheets, refrigerators, towels, and clothing are in-season retail. This is the phase where most manufacturers require the retailers that carry their products to follow recommended pricing (called MSRP or MAP). The bulk of product sales and correspondingly margin are made in this phase, by manufacturers and retailers alike.

For example, if you want to buy a PlayStation 2, you can go to Sears, Best Buy, Electronics Boutique, Circuit City, and any number of other stores and find it for the same price. Special bundles and perhaps different services will be available, but basically, the product is the same price at all outlets.

■ **Phase 3—End of life.** The end of a product's life is usually caused by the introduction of a new product in the category by the manufacturer or sometimes by a competitor. At this point of the life cycle, manufacturers and retailers alike are interested in getting rid of the product as quickly as possible to make way for the hot new product. Also, Phase 3 product is typically sold at cost or at a small loss, because consumer demand shifts from the older product to the newer one, causing sellers to use a great price to tempt consumers into buying an older, out-of-style product.

For example, when Mr. Coffee comes out with a new and improved coffee maker (let's call it the Mr. Coffee 3000), it usually replaces the older model (the Mr. Coffee 2000). The same is true for autos, consumer electronics, computers, clothes, and more. In this example, the Mr. Coffee 2000 would most likely be put on "end of life" by the manufacturer and no longer sold. Retailers would take this as a cue to mark down the product and make way for the Mr. Coffee 3000. You can conceptualize versions of products "pushing" others through the phases of the life cycle. When the Mr. Coffee 3000 is in Phase 1 (introduction), it causes the 2000 to go into Phase 3 (end of life). Once the 3000 makes it into Phase 2 (in-season retail), that will push the 2000 into Phase 4 (liquidation).

Figure 4.2 illustrates how new products can push older products through the life cycle.

- **Phase 4—Liquidation.** At this point of the product life cycle, there are overstocks of the product, refurbished units, and general remnants working their way through the system. Both the manufacturer and the retailer actively try to avoid ending up with Phase 4 product, because it usually is sold at a very large loss. Industry metrics suggest that liquidation product sells for 10 to 20% of cost—in other words, for a loss of 80 to 90%. Given this data point, you can see why liquidation product is a hot potato. In fact, in a perfect world, retailers and manufacturers would eliminate Phase 4 entirely. Unfortunately, because consumers are human, Phase 4 is unavoidable. Today's must-have product can just as easily turn into tomorrow's liquidation item.

  For example, one retail company a couple of years ago bet big that leather pants would be the hot trend for women's clothing for the fall and winter. The company

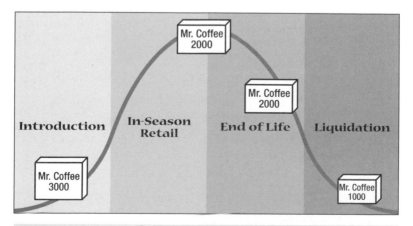

FIGURE 4.2   New products drive older ones through the life cycle

bought tons of leather pants (literally) and stocked them in thousands of stores. Unfortunately, the company guessed wrong, and consumers in only select cities in the Northeast found the leather pants appealing. Within two months, the company realized its error and was liquidating leather pants through every possible means, at a significant loss. This one buying mistake almost put the company out of business, but from a consumer's point of view, it was a great opportunity to get leather pants at a deep discount.

Now that we've established the product life cycle, let's look at how it relates to eBay.

3 UNDERSTAND AND LEVERAGE THE EBAY SWEET SPOTS

Products in different parts of their life cycle will perform differently on eBay. In fact, eBay has two clear "sweet spots," as illustrated in Figure 4.3.

The eBay curve in Figure 4.3 shows sweet spots that are stages of the product life cycle. They can guide you to those products that will do better on eBay, as compared to products in a different phase of their life cycle. The two primary sweet spots for eBay in the product life cycle are these:

■ **Phase 1—Introduction.** When products are introduced and their supply cannot keep up with demand, eBay provides a unique opportunity to profit from the supply/de-

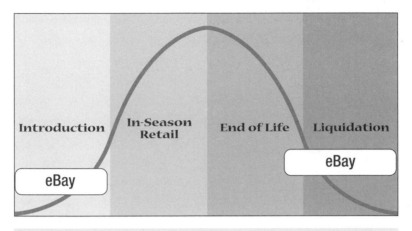

FIGURE 4.3   The eBay "sweet spots" in the product life cycle

mand imbalance. For example, you may recall when the PlayStation 2 and competing Xbox game consoles were introduced, those items sold on eBay for anywhere from 10 to 100% above retail prices. Also, every holiday season, there are some hot toys that sell out at department stores but are available on eBay.

The "introduction" cycle is so strong on eBay that some manufacturers have started launching their products on eBay and are developing eBay-only products. For example, two collectible companies, Ty and Hummel, have developed eBay-only versions of their products. Also, Motorola recently launched a new phone, the v70, on eBay. While the proceeds went to charity, Motorola was able to generate considerable excitement for the product, which carried through to the "in-season retail" phase of the product's life cycle.

■ Phase 4—Liquidation. If you've been selling for any time, you know that eBay buyers love a deal. The auction format feeds into the "deal hunting" and makes buyers feel as if they are playing a game, competing for the best deals.

Also, eBay buyers frequently will buy a product that's a little bit older or not so cutting edge to get a deal. Liquidation product is the perfect product to source for eBay.

What about the other parts of the product life cycle? Most of the time, in-season product will not do well on eBay. There are many reasons why:

- **Product availability.** In-season product is typically snapped up by the largest of retailers, such as Best Buy and Wal-Mart. Even if you can get some of this product, the big players acquire product at such significant discounts that they are able to undersell a small business. Additionally, in-season retail products typically have very tight margins, in the range of 5 to 20%. Given that you will be paying eBay 5 to 7% and paying a payment processor 2 to 3%, there is little or no margin left to cover expenses.

- **eBay buyers.** As mentioned, eBay buyers are looking for a great deal. That usually equates to 20 to 50% or more off of retail pricing.

- **Price comparison.** When buying in-season retail product, most buyers are looking for the latest and greatest, and they are willing to pay more for that product. Correspondingly, they are looking for services such as extended warranty programs, free shipping, free accessories, and so on. Most buyers will use a comparison-shopping engine or compare prices themselves among the off-line and online retailers offering the product. eBay doesn't show up in these comparisons because many buyers don't check eBay first for the hottest items. Also, eBay is not able to send auction listings to comparison-shopping engines such as Shopping.com and Yahoo! Shopping.

As with anything, there are exceptions to the rule. Occasionally, a seller will find an in-season retail item on sale in his or her region, buy it, and sell the product to someone in a different part of the country for a profit.

End-of-life product can also be difficult to sell on eBay. The primary problem with end-of-life product is there is frequently so much that it is sold by the truckload, or by the thousands. Though it's possible to sell a great deal of product on eBay, selling thousands of anything in a short time can be a challenge. As you will see in pricing, there are trade-offs between the price you achieve and the number of units of a given SKU you are able to move. We generally counsel most eBay sellers to avoid product that has just hit the end of its life, because there typically will be a great deal of product on the market for a month or two, as most retailers and manufacturers push out the product in bulk—which can create a short-term glut or oversupply.

The exceptions are if you are able to get smaller quantities (hundreds, not thousands) of end-of-life product or if you buy thousands and have other means of selling the items. Another exception would be using a middleman who can break up the products from thousands to hundreds and resell them to you in smaller lots. The downside of this last option is that usually the eBay market still becomes flooded with the items, resulting in significant pricing pressure.

Applying the eBay Sweet Spots to Your Business

The next time you are sourcing product or looking to get into a new category, you should think about the eBay sweet spots in the product life cycle. What are some introduction or end-of-life products in the category that you can source and on which you can make your margin targets? Is there any end-of-life product available? If so, is there already a large amount of the product on eBay? Is there too much for you to be able to sell what you need to sell?

Another angle is to look at the product you are sourcing today and think about how you can experiment with both sides of the product life cycle. Perhaps you could source some newer product and some slightly older product and run a test to see how those two new groups of product do compared to your current product base.

For example, if you sell MP3 players, it's important strategically to start thinking about the product life cycle. You may find that although you have had some success with relatively new MP3 players, once you experiment with older MP3 players, you actually make more margin and can source the products more easily, and so on.

Product Seasons and Regionalization

Many categories of products have "seasons" that drive where products are on the product life cycle. Additionally, consumers in various regions of the United States (and the world) may buy products in different patterns. The best example of these phenomena is apparel (or clothing). Apparel has four to six seasons. Buyers are frequently keyed into the seasons and buy in front of them. Also, buyers in various parts of the country behave differently, because they have dissimilar seasons and because there is a variety of regional tastes. For example, buyers in New York start buying fall and winter clothes in August and September, whereas buyers in Florida and California are looking for fall and winter clothes in November and December (if at all!).

Seasonality and regionalization can dramatically affect your business. Most likely you won't be able to sell artificial Christmas trees in July, and you will have to hold on to highly seasonal product for six to twelve months until that season rolls around again. Sometimes regionalization can work to your advantage. For example, we work with a seller of snowboards and water skis that can drive year-round sales of both product types by strategically shipping internationally for the winter items in summer. And they are able to offer the "always warm" regions their summer items. Florida and California have large concentrations of eBay buyers and are responsible for most of this seller's "off-season" summer goods sales. So, with eBay, you can sell snowboards in July and water skis in December if you understand and embrace the intricacies of product seasons and regionalization.

Product Depth and Width

As you think about your product strategy, one possibility for expanding your business is to source more of what you already sell successfully. This strategy is certainly appealing, because of the immediate economies of scale. You need only one picture and one description for everything you sell, so why not sell 1,000 instead of 10? Also, you can make your business more predictable by knowing ahead of time that you need to source X number of a certain SKU every month, versus having to start from scratch month after month.

Unfortunately, the demand on eBay can handle only a finite amount of product supply. In fact, as you start to add more quantity to what you're already selling, you will find that one symptom of an oversupply in product is that average selling prices (both yours and those of your competitors) will come down substantially.

Another product strategy that many eBay businesses adopt to increase sales is to offer more SKUs. Usually, sellers start by offering more SKUs in the same category in which they are currently selling. Once they feel that category is saturated, they move on to entirely different categories. Frequently, new expansion categories are related to the first, or core, category.

For example, if you are a video game seller, you can expand your business from PlayStation 2 games to Xbox games, Game Boy games, and so on. Then you may actually expand into video game consoles, or perhaps other media, or maybe even something entirely different, such as auto parts.

Every seller has a different product depth-and-width sweet spot. For example, we know sellers who offer 5,000 SKUs for sale but have only have one or maybe two of each. Still, there are other sellers who offer only 50 SKUs and sell hundreds of these hot items a month.

Let's look at a rule of thumb to help you think about your goals and how product width and depth factor into them. In this example, we will use eBay averages; but once you understand the average example, you should be able to run the numbers for your specific eBay vitals.

SellerX has the following eBay business vitals and goals:

- **Current GMS:** **$10,000 per month**
- **ASP:** **$50**

- **CR:** **50%**

- **Items listed per month:** **400**

- **Items sold per month:** **200**

- **Unique SKUs:** **20**

- **Average number sold per month per SKU:** **10**

- **Goal:** **$30,000 per month sales**

Given these data points for this eBay business, here are some thoughts on product depth and width and how to use them to drive the business.

At $30,000 per month in sales, assuming the seller is able to keep the ASP at $50, the seller will need to post 1,200 listings a month and sell 600 of them.

Our recommendation would be first to look at depth by working with the original SKUs. So we would suggest analyzing the initial set of 20 SKUs: see which of them are selling above or at the $50 ASP, try to double the volume of those until the ASP drops 10%, and then hold steady at that volume. Then run the same experiment for the other SKUs in the original 20. Another way of figuring out which of the original SKUs are most likely to support more depth is to look at the number of bids per SKU. Items that receive more than five bids per listing indicate strong demand and lack of supply in the marketplace. SKUs that receive fewer than five bids per listing are more balanced and will not support as much depth.

Most likely, in this example, about half of the SKUs will be able to double or more in depth, which should drive an immediate increase of $5,000 to $10,000 in sales. Thus, total sales resulting from working on the product depth are $15,000 to $20,000 per month. By increasing the depth, we have raised the average depth per SKU from 10 to 15–20 (let's assume 20).

Next, we would recommend looking at the products with the greatest depth from the original SKUs and trying to replicate the success of those original SKUs by sourcing more product that can also be sold in depth. For the goal of selling 600 items a month at 20 deep, we will need 30 SKUs. We already have 20, so we need to source 10 to 15 new SKUs. We recommend oversourcing, because with new SKUs, you may be able to anticipate the potential depth on a monthly basis, but you won't know for sure until you start selling the new SKUs and get some results.

If you are sourcing 10 to 15 new SKUs, we recommend using that opportunity to expand outside of your current category, if possible. Once you source the products and get a month or two of data under your belt, you'll be able to go back and source product smarter.

In conclusion, in this example, we showed how to take SellerX from $10,000 per month in sales to $30,000 per month in sales by initially focusing on product depth and then focusing on product width.

In Chapters 5 and 6 (on pricing and promotion), we'll provide more insight into how to gauge the demand of various products, which will give you a better ability to anticipate depth.

Product Mix

As we mentioned previously, the mix of your product is another aspect of product that can be used to drive your business. As you analyze the product piece of your eBay business, spend some time looking at the mix. One metric you may want to introduce is the number of broad and narrow categories your items are in. Examples of broad categories are books and digital cameras. A narrow category is video games: Sony PlayStation 2 versus Xbox. Books and digital cameras are broad because you can add new categories that are different within the category. For example, in digital cameras you can add accessories, memory cards, different megapixel-range models, and so on. This will help you as you expand the width of your product selection.

Another aspect of product mix you should consider is accessories or up-sells. If you sell a product for which the buyer may need some accessory (and almost all products fall into this category), this is a great way to increase your sales without having to do much extra work. In fact, frequently the most economical way to achieve this increase is via a checkout up-sell or an eBay Store.

For example, let's say you sell collectible comic books. Why not also offer comic book collecting supplies? At checkout, you can offer the user the chance to buy your top four to ten accessories. Also, in your comic book auction listings, you can have a spot that says something like "Looking for accessories? Click here." The link will take the user into your eBay Store, where you can have inexpensive listings that stay there until inventory runs out. Usually, it does not make sense to list accessories or supplies in the auction or fixed-price formats because of the higher listing fees and the lower conversion rates of these items.

When looking at up-sells, another metric that's important to keep an eye on is the *attach rate*. This is defined as the percentage of orders that include an up-sold item as well as the core item. Depending on the category, we have seen attach rates as low as 2% and as high as 30%. The electronics categories tend to have the highest attach rates. For example, we have a digital camera seller who up-sells a high-margin accessory literally one-third of the time.

Let's look at an example of how up-sales can drive your business. Assume you have a $50 ASP and sell 200 items a month ($10,000 per month GMS) and make $1,000 in net margin a month, or $5 an item. Now let's assume you are able to sell an accessory on 15% of the orders. The accessories are $20 ASP and also have a $5 margin. You would sell 15% × 200 = 30 accessories for an additional $600 in GMS and an additional $150 in margin. In this example, up-selling increased GMS only 6% but raised net margin 15%, which boosts the overall profitability of your model.

Most sellers experience similar benefits when they start selling margin-rich accessories as up-sells for their core items.

Product Classification

Once your eBay business gets into the range of $50,000 a month and up, it will become hard to remember the details of all the product you have purchased, how long you have had it, and what you sold it for. Inevitably, you will start to have longer inventory cycles, and you will need a system for keeping your inventory organized, so you can sell it more efficiently.

At this level, we have found it helpful to think in terms of three classes or classifications of product:

1. **Class A product.** Recently acquired product in which you have a good bit of investment and that you need to sell at a price no less than your cost.

2. **Class B product.** Product that you may have had on hand for a while and need to start moving to make way for new product—or to avoid having to take a loss on the product.

3. **Class C product.** Liquidation product. Product that you have not been able to move and may need to sell for whatever the market will bear. Class C product is to be avoided or minimized, but any business getting near the million-dollar-a-year mark will end up with some Class C product, so it's best to recognize this and plan for it.

As an exercise, look at your inventory (either physically walk around and inspect it or review a printout if you have one) and try to put it into one of these three categories. What percentage mix do you have? In our experience, the typical mix is 60/30/10 of Class A/B/C product for sellers in the segment of $50,000 a month and up. Is this in line with what you have?

If you have more Class C product than 10% and more Class B than 30%, this can indicate that either your pricing strategy has problems or you are not sourcing strong product—or both. The next chapter covers pricing and how you can use these product classifications to drive pricing decisions, as well as sourcing decisions.

Sourcing Product

All of the aspects of product discussed so far should be considered as you perform one of the most important functions of your eBay business: sourcing product. As you look to source product, you should consider the following:

- **Product life cycle. Remember that the eBay sweet spot is product at the start of its life cycle (that is, introduction) and toward the end of the life cycle (liquidation). For introduction products, try to anticipate hot products and buy them in bulk before they become hot. Although this is a risky strategy, if you are good at it, the margins are significant. On liquidation product, try to source products that are still interesting to consumers even if something newer or better has recently come on the market. You should be prepared to sell the liquidation products for a significant discount (such as 30 to 50% off) from the retail/street price, so source your product with this in mind.**

With liquidation product, the more services you can provide, the more types of product you can source. For example, if your eBay business is able to test equipment to make sure it is working and perform light repair, then you can source "like new" or potentially damaged goods. The key to these services is making sure you are able to make profit on any additional services you put in. For example, if on average you buy a "needs repair" laptop for $500 and are able to sell it for $800, make sure you are not adding more than $300 in cost to the product, and that you are hitting your margin targets. Given the increasing prices for labor, it is very easy to lose money when performing any level of service, so monitor this very carefully.

- **Product depth and width.** When you source product, pay particular attention to the depth of the product you are sourcing. One of the traps to avoid is the "buy-too-much" trap. Product suppliers frequently lower the price for product when you purchase higher quantities. This arrangement sounds good, but when you are making such large purchases, remember that eBay can handle only a certain volume before your ASP begins to fall significantly. Unless you are getting a great deal or have other channels (as we discuss in Chapter 7, "Placement"), you should stock no more than two to three months in depth for eBay-only SKUs.

- **Product mix.** Additionally, when sourcing, take the opportunity to expand into accessories and potentially new categories. When possible, try to leverage your customer base by staying close to your current category. But don't be afraid to try something completely new if you can do so in a relatively low-risk way.

Product Source Ideas

Most sellers treat their product sources as the most confidential part of their business. In fact, many sellers will be glad to talk about their GMS, margins, ASP, CR, and other metrics, but when you bring up where they source products, they clam up.

I've found that many sellers start in a particular category buying from a retailer—usually in the discount bin or at a store such as Big Lots. Then once they've established that a product is successful on eBay, they call the manufacturer to find out who the distributors are.

Once they have the name of the distributor, they call to see if they can be a reseller for the product. Sellers generally quote pretty large volumes they will be able to sell, in order to get the distributor interested.

The key is not to be shy. You would be surprised what you can discover if you pick up the phone, call the manufacturer, tell them you are an end-of-life/liquidation retailer, and explain that you would like to start carrying their end-of-life products. Usually, retailers and manufacturers have someone in sales or marketing responsible for selling excess inventory, and that person is usually glad to add you to the list of regular inventory available for purchase or bid.

In fact, many manufacturers use dynamic pricing in their liquidation models. For example, Motorola hosts a monthly auction for qualified resellers to bid on end-of-life cell-phone inventory. Many retailers deal with excess inventory on a regional basis. For example, one eBay seller sources inventory from the local Bloomingdale's department store, which is the Bloomingdale's facility for the entire central United States.

In fact, especially scrappy sellers work with their sources to secure exclusive relationships. These typically require certain volume commitments and other complex arrangements. However, securing an exclusive with a great product source is the smartest strategic maneuver you can make.

Here is a list of potential sources for you to consider. For each source, we know sellers who source from them regularly. Beware of the numerous scams out there, which offer books of sources for $10 to $500. Typically, these books simply list distributors in various industries, or they offer other information that you could just as easily find by using Google, your local phone book, or the industrial guides at your local library.

Retailers

The following retailers have regular wholesale end-of-life liquidations of various products:

- **CompUSA.** This computer retailer frequently holds liquidation auctions at http://www.compusawholesale.com.

- **Techliquidators.** A top electronics retailer that hosts closed-bid auctions for products sold in lots at http://www.techliquidators.com.

- **RetailExchange.** A network of retail liquidators operated by the largest and oldest retail liquidator: Gordon Brothers. At http://www.retailexchange.com.

- **Genco.** Many top retailers utilize Genco to handle their open-box returns. Genco sorts the goods and then makes them available to sell in bulk to resellers. You can see what's available here: http://www.genco.com/eb2b. Only registered users can bid.

- **Big Lots.** Big Lots sells online wholesale lots at http://www.biglotswholesale.com.

Wholesalers

With wholesalers, you need to be cautious, because many require you to pay a membership fee before you can even see the prices. This requirement can turn out to be a scam, so check that the site actually has inventory you will get to see—not an overpriced booklet with information of questionable value.

- **Liquidation.com.** A wholesaler that takes truckloads of goods and breaks them down into smaller lots for businesses such as eBay sellers. This source is very well known. When you buy product here, you will be competing with lots of other eBay businesses, so buy smart. Liquidation.com recently opened up their marketplace to third-party sellers. Be careful to learn as much as possible about a third-party seller before you buy. We have heard some buyers express concern about the shipping fees and potential buyer premiums at this site.

- **Overstockb2b.com.** Here a famous end-of-life e-tailer, Overstock.com, sells its overstock to resellers. You would be surprised how much of this product ends up on eBay.

- **eBay Wholesale.** eBay has added wholesale categories at http://pages.ebay.com/catindex/catwholesale.html. This is perhaps the best-known product source, so the prices are rarely very attractive. eBay Wholesale is useful to see the average prices paid on items such as CDs, DVDs, video games, and anything you may be interested in, so you can use those prices as a target when you buy elsewhere.

- **Surplus.net.** A site that aggregates the items for sale from hundreds of liquidators around the world. Buyer beware.

- **Closeout.net.** An aggregation of wholesale closeouts. There is a variety of sellers here, and little if any checking is done on them, so again, buyer beware.

- **Wholesale411.com.** An information site with lists of wholesale sources. Some sellers have reported great luck using this list; others have found it not to be trustworthy. Once more, buyer beware.

Manufacturers

The following is just a sampling of manufacturers that sell their excess/refurbished/end-of-life inventory to resellers. Typically, you can call the manufacturer and ask to speak to someone in sales; they will point you in the right direction.

- **Motorola**
  http://motorolawholesale.channeladvisor.com
  Buy excess and refurbished cell phones and accessories directly from Motorola.

- **Nokia**
  http://www.nokiaprivatemarket.com
  Buy cell phones and accessories directly from Nokia.

- **IBM**
  http://partnerchoiceauctions.channeladvisor.com
  Buy excess and refurbished IBM desktops and laptops.

GlacierBayDVD

Seller: glacierbaydvd (130523 ☆) m⊜ ⊜

After achieving their goal of becoming the top DVD business on eBay, GlacierBayDVD isn't stopping there; they have now opened other stores to dramatically expand the availability of Glacier Bay products. At the time of this writing, GlacierBayDVD is the number-two seller on all of eBay, based on feedback, and they should become number one before the 2004 holiday season.

We chose GlacierBayDVD for this chapter's case study, which focuses on products, because unlike many sellers, they have decided to crack one of the toughest categories on eBay: DVDs. They wouldn't rest until they were the top seller. Based on that success, you will see they have plans for even more interesting product decisions.

eBay Vitals

- GMS: $300,000–$400,000 per month
- ASP: $15–$20
- CR: 30–40%
- Feedback: 99.0%
- Ships more than 1,000 DVDs a day

Background

In 1999, Randy Smythe's son was an avid Pokemon card collector. To help him build his collection, Randy started buying Pokemon cards in bulk. His son kept the cards needed for the collection and Randy sold the remnants individually on eBay. This quickly became a very profitable venture (and Randy's son developed an awesome collection).

After the Pokemon experience, Randy was an adept eBay seller, and he realized that he could potentially make more money by selling on eBay than in his "day job." Randy tested a variety of products and, after buying several cases of DVDs, found they did very well for him.

GlacierBayDVD was born in late 1999. At inception, Randy not only decided that he would open up a DVD store on eBay, but also that his goal would be to dominate the category.

Today GlacierBayDVD employs 12 people and plans to open several new "Glacier Bay" stores. As you can guess, it's Randy's goal to be the top seller in those categories as well, and it will be interesting to see if their success can be duplicated in non-DVD categories.

GlacierBayDVD is located in California.

Figure 4.4 shows GlacierBayDVD's About Me page. Figure 4.5 shows one of GlacierBayDVD's live items for sale.

GlacierBayDVD and Product

When experimenting with those first cases of DVDs, Randy realized that DVDs are an interesting product because there are so many titles and potential ways that buyers can discover the DVDs they are looking for. Randy decided his product strategy early on: he wanted to have the widest selection of DVDs on eBay, so that when a buyer was looking for *any* DVD, he or she couldn't help but find GlacierBayDVD.

Others questioned this strategy, urging GlacierBayDVD to expand into new categories early, but Randy held to the original strategy—and it has paid off handsomely.

At the time of this writing, GlacierBayDVD regularly offers more than 10,000 titles for sale on eBay. Yes, 10,000 titles. The most popular titles sell more than 100 copies a month. GlacierBayDVD has developed sophisticated inventory-sourcing systems to anticipate and stock popular titles and maintain the broad GlacierBayDVD selection.

FIGURE 4.4 The GlacierBayDVD About Me page

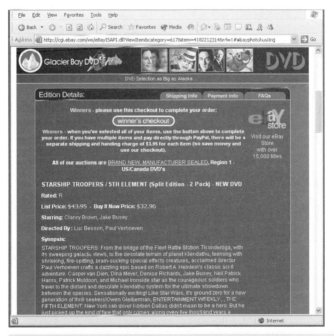

FIGURE 4.5 A GlacierBayDVD item for sale

To help buyers find titles, GlacierBayDVD provides several mechanisms. For example, they maintain an eBay Store that displays the products by category, such as drama, action, and so on. Additionally, GlacierBayDVD fully utilizes the eBay item-specifics/attributes feature and has implemented a custom search that lets buyers search by title, actor, or director. You can see the search box in Figure 4.4.

Interestingly, recalling the product life cycle, GlacierBayDVD has found that the best products are the end-of-life selections. Introductory product for DVDs doesn't enjoy an eBay sweet spot the way other products do, because supply is plentiful and many top retailers discount new releases substantially. Thus, GlacierBayDVD's product strategy focuses on the mature product that's most likely no longer available in retail outlets, but which consumers may still be looking for on eBay.

Other Strategies of Interest

Randy has developed an interesting pricing strategy, based on the discovery that most buyers want instant gratification. All listings have a BIN that is determined by a proprietary formula, which ensures not only that GlacierBayDVD achieves its margin targets, but also that the BIN buyer gets a great deal. In fact, the original retail price is generally shown in the listing so the buyer can figure out how much he or she will be saving! Opening bids are also set by a formula developed over the years by GlacierBayDVD, which balances margin requirements with the conversion rate to optimize eBay fees.

Another great strategy developed by GlacierBayDVD is flat-rate shipping. Each package that GlacierBayDVD sends out is $3.95, regardless of the number of DVDs. Once buyers realize this, they add on more DVDs like crazy, which also keeps the customer loyal to GlacierBayDVD. Other sellers might offer lower prices, but buyers eager to save dramatically on shipping stay with GlacierBayDVD.

In fact, many other DVD sellers on eBay use shipping as a profit center. Their shipping charges are in the range of $5 or more, which makes GlacierBayDVD look that much more attractive.

Chapter 4 Summary

Product life cycle—As new products are released, they mature through a well-defined product life cycle. As a consumer, you may already have been somewhat involved in this cycle. As an eBay businessperson, it is essential to understand the product life cycle so you can target the best product to source and sell on eBay. The four phases of the product life cycle are introduction, in-season retail, end of life, and liquidation.

KEY CONCEPTS

In this chapter, we explored in detail the first *P* of the Five P's strategic framework: product. In an eBay business, choosing which products to carry (and all other product decisions) is one of the most strategic decisions you will make.

After introducing the product life cycle and reviewing the four phases, we explained the eBay sweet spots of the product life cycle: introduction and liquidation. Introduction product rarely becomes available in quantity and requires a great amount of time to locate. Therefore, we recommend a focus on liquidation and end-of-life product.

When considering how to source liquidation and end-of-life product, it's important to have a clear understanding of the depth of product (inventory per SKU) and width of product (the number of SKUs) that your business can handle. Our recommendation is to focus on understanding the depth your business can sustain by testing some of your current SKUs incrementally. Once you have determined the right depth, then you can start to expand, adding SKUs at the depth you have determined. Experimenting with SKU depth and width can dramatically increase your eBay business, with minimal effort.

In addition to product depth and width, we recommend experimenting with the product mix. For example, one best

Chapter 4 Summary

practice is to experiment with adding accessories that complement the core products you offer. Accessory sales can give your business a very rapid margin boost. In addition to accessory sales, another best practice is to consider expanding into new categories that are similar to your existing ones—or if your business can handle some trial and error, try some completely new categories of product.

Once your business achieves sales in excess of $50,000 (and maybe sooner, depending on your ASP), it will be helpful to mentally or formally divide your products into three classifications: Class A, Class B, and Class C. When we cover price, in Chapter 5, this methodology will allow you to implement a variety of pricing strategies.

Finally, all the product strategies described here should be taken into consideration when it is time to source product. Your product sources are the most confidential and valuable information you have as an eBay business, so you should guard them closely and work diligently to expand them. Securing an exclusive distribution deal can be one of the best strategic moves you can make in your business.

Finally, we provided a list of known sources. Unfortunately, the best sources are those you can't find in a book (even this one), so you'll most likely have to roll up your sleeves and start hunting sources.

EXERCISES

1. What is the largest quantity of a SKU that you have ever sold per month?

2. What are your sources of product? What can you do to expand your sources?

3. Have a discussion with your best source about exclusivity.

FIVE

Price

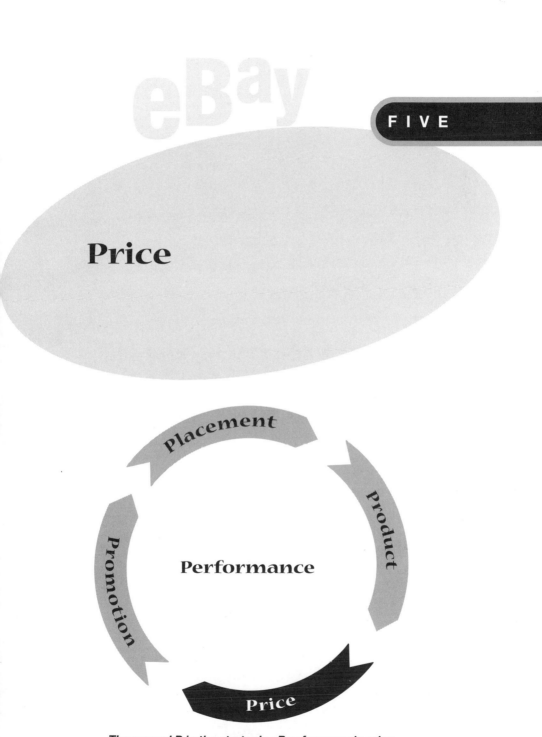

The second P in the strategic eBay framework: price

he second *P* of the Five P's is *price*. When refer-
ring to price, we're not talking only about the
price at which you sell things on eBay; once you
maximize the selling price, the acquisition price
becomes equally important. The difference between the
buying and the selling price determines your gross margin,
which is the primary driver of your net margin. In this
chapter, we examine first the prices you achieve when selling on eBay, and we explore various strategies to maximize
the price. Then we look at how to take that selling price
knowledge and apply it to the buying side as well.

4 UNDERSTAND THE EBAY PRICE/VELOCITY CURVE

In Chapter 4, we introduced the strategic concepts of
product width and depth. We also alluded to the fact
that price and quantity of inventory are also related. In
fact, on eBay, there exists a clear relationship between the
price at which you sell your goods and the quantity you
can sell over a defined amount of time. This is called *product velocity*. The more you can sell in a time frame, the
more product velocity you have. Figure 5.1 shows the eBay
price/velocity curve. Note that in mapping this curve, we
assume that demand remains the same and that no promotions or other special efforts take place.

Figure 5.1 illustrates the basic principle that you can sell
anything on eBay, but the price may not be what you want.
The price/velocity curve shows that there is a very important trade-off between the price you achieve for the items
(also called the yield) and the quantity of the item you

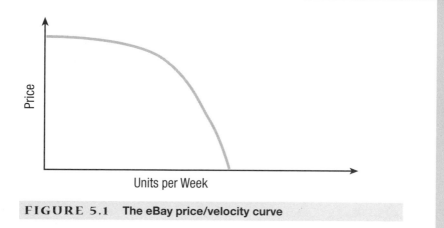

FIGURE 5.1 **The eBay price/velocity curve**

want to sell. In fact, this makes common sense. The more you want to sell of something, the lower the price you need to accept, to move the higher volumes. Conversely, the higher the price you want to achieve, the fewer you will need to sell.

If you've ever taken an economics class, the eBay price/velocity curve probably looks familiar: it reflects the basic interactions of supply and demand. The key concept to understand is that on eBay, without your doing any promotions or anything special, the demand in the marketplace for various SKUs is relatively fixed—demand doesn't change much over a 30-day to 60-day period. Thus, the only other variable at work is supply. You control supply, and your competitors control supply.

Let's walk through an example using the price/velocity curve. Let's say you have a very large quantity of a SKU— say, 10,000 units. Figure 5.2 shows three data points that illustrate the price/velocity trade-off.

At the first data point, the SKU sells for $150; at that price, the seller can sell 10 a week. At the second data point, the velocity has increased significantly, to 20 items a

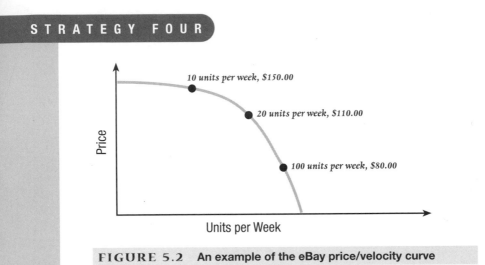

FIGURE 5.2 An example of the eBay price/velocity curve

week, but the price has fallen to $110. At the final data point, the velocity has again increased to 100 items per week, but in concert, the price achieved drops to only $80.

Applying the eBay Price/Velocity Curve

In Chapter 4, we recommended growing depth first and then expanding the width of product SKUs. Given the dynamics of the eBay price/velocity curve, you can go a step further and actually use trial and error to start understanding the price/velocity curve for each of your SKUs.

To do this, you need to figure out where you are on the curve by measuring how many of your SKUs are selling now, and at what velocity. Once you have this first data point, you can start increasing the volume of listings and see what effect this has on the ASP and velocity. After a month, you should have three or four data points and be able to understand the price/velocity curve dynamics for your test SKU.

Armed with this information, you can make important strategic decisions based on your goals.

For example, SellerX has tested a SKU and found these data points:

PRICE	VELOCITY (ITEMS SOLD PER WEEK)
$150	10
$120	20
$100	40
$ 80	60

Currently SellerX is selling 10 of the SKU per month at $150 each. SellerX's goal is to increase monthly absolute gross margin (not a percentage). The SKU cost the seller $100 at current volumes (40 per month), but if SellerX can increase sales to more than 100 a month, the cost decreases to $85 each.

Given this information, SellerX evaluates three scenarios:

■ Scenario 1: **Low volume/high margin. The item sells for $150 by 40 units a month, with cost of $100, for total gross margin of 40 × $50 = $2,000.**

■ Scenario 2: **Medium volume/medium margin. The item sells for $120 by 80 units a month, with cost of $100, for total gross margin of 80 × $20 = $1,600.**

■ Scenario 3: **High volume/low margin. The item sells for $100 but with 160 units a month, thus lowering the cost to $85, for a gross margin of 160 × $15 = $2,400.**

Before reading the results, would you have guessed that Scenario 3 made the most sense? These decisions are frequently made by very experienced sellers who are somewhat more emotionally driven than data driven. Most sellers would rather walk on glass rather than purposely lower their ASPs. The important thing to realize is that many of these decisions are counterintuitive, so you have to cast emotion aside and rely on the data to make the best decisions.

Not every scenario will play out with the high volume/lower margin approach as optimal. Once you understand the price/velocity trade-offs for some of your SKUs, you will start to get a much better feel for your sweet spot in the market and in your category. Soon your intuition will become stronger, you will be able to make rapid decisions based on your knowledge of the price/velocity cycle, and you will be able to leverage that knowledge strategically for your eBay business.

Finally, as this example illustrates, when you know the price/velocity curve for your products, you will be better able to negotiate pricing when you source products. You will be able to go for volume pricing, knowing what the volumes will do for your ASP and margins.

Caution: Falling ASPs

The number one complaint we hear about eBay from sellers is that their ASPs are decreasing. Ironically, once you dig into the problem with an understanding of the eBay price/velocity curve, you see that the sellers themselves are responsible for the ASP decrease, *not* eBay. In fact, blaming eBay for something like this makes no sense. There can be only a couple of reasons for falling ASPs:

■ **Competition.** Competitors are selling the same product for less, thus taking buyers to lower prices compared to your price, which forces you to lower your price to sell your items. Note that eBay buyers are pretty sophisticated, so the competition may come directly from eBay sellers or indirectly from another venue either off-line or online. Competing sellers on eBay may be competing with you not only on price; in today's environment, it's equally as likely they are out-promoting you (which we'll cover in the next chapter).

- **Self-competition.** Self-competition is a *very* important concept for every eBay seller to understand. Look again at Figure 5.1 and you will see self-competition at work. Most sellers don't realize that there is a definite, clear relationship between price and velocity, so they flood the market with product. When they do so, the result is to drive down the ASP for the SKU and sometimes for entire categories of products. The seller frequently blames eBay for not supplying enough buyers when in fact the seller is his own worst enemy.

  The best case study of self-competition is a seller that acquired literally thousands of Palm PDAs. The seller was aware of eBay's "ten-listing rule," which limits each seller to ten listings for the same SKU at any given time. To get around the rule, he opened an additional five stores on eBay and started posting the SKUs with ten listings, some Dutch, on all five stores. Within weeks, this single seller had driven the ASP for all Palm units down more than 15%—in fact, well below what he had bought the thousands of Palms for! When the business filed for bankruptcy, they blamed eBay and decreasing ASPs for their failure, not self-competition.

- **Buyer change.** Sometimes ASPs can decrease because a certain item becomes less attractive to buyers. Buyers can lose interest in a product for any number of reasons, but usually there are external influences, such as seasonality, regionalism, and new product introductions.

  Buyers change the most in the computer category, because of the rapid pace of innovation. For example, every 18 months or so, Intel announces a new chip set. Within 15 to

30 days of these announcements, the ASPs for older technologies drop on the order of 5 to 10%! Thus, the computer category's ASPs decrease 1 to 2% on a quarterly and sometimes monthly basis.

This example shows how important it can be to understand the external influences that can affect your sales. You must keep a finger on the pulse of these changes. For example, the smart computer seller knows that Intel usually announces new technology at COMDEX and will clear out inventory well before this event. Savvy sellers even use the announcement as a way to buy liquidation product after COMDEX. The naive seller can hit a worst-case scenario: buying a bunch of product before COMDEX and having to take a significant loss when the product is made less attractive by an industry announcement.

- **Some of the above.** Usually when you encounter decreasing ASPs, any number of and possibly all of the preceding factors may be at play.

Researching Decreasing ASPs

If you encounter a significant decrease in ASPs, you can research the previous reasons pretty easily to ascertain what could be at work. Here are the steps you can take to research what may be driving down your ASPs:

1. Check current listings and completed items on eBay to see what the competition is up to. If you have data on the top search terms for your SKU, use them; if not, take a best guess at two to five search terms that buyers may be using to find your items. What prices are the competitors selling for? Are there any listings that really stand out from the others? Are there any BINs or fixed-price listings that are lower than your selling price?

2. If you don't find anything there, then you should search a couple of the top e-commerce/shopping engines to see what "street" prices are for the item. At the very least, you should check these sites:

- www.amazon.com
- www.overstock.com
- www.shopping.com
- www.froogle.com
- www.pricegrabber.com
- www.pricescan.com

These six searches will cover most online and off-line competitors.

3. If you have reached this step and still can't find what has caused your ASPs to decrease, then you should check for news on the manufacturer and model and category you are selling. Perhaps a new product has been released, or some other external influences are at work.

The best way to demonstrate ASP research is through a real-world example. In this example, SellerX has noticed a significant decrease in the ASP for a handheld GPS—the Garmin eTrex Legend (with 8MB memory). This item has sold briskly for $189 over the last several months, and now the item fetches $160 or less—a 16% price decrease! The seller's cost on these items is $150, so as you can imagine, he is very concerned about this dramatic decrease. SellerX typically sells 30 of these a week, and it has been a great-performing SKU until the decrease.

First, SellerX goes to eBay to see what the competition is up to. He learns that the top search for this item is "garmin etrex legend." Figure 5.3 shows a sample eBay search for this term.

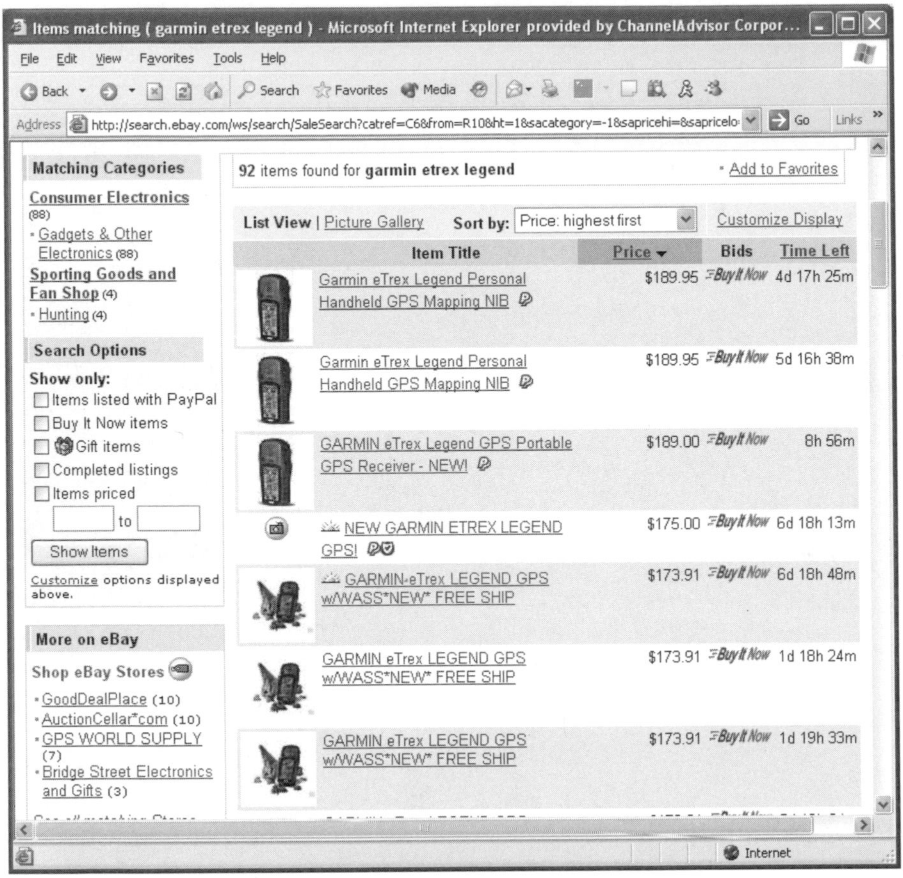

FIGURE 5.3   A sample eBay search

Of the 92 results, the lowest BIN is $167, which is Seller-X. As you can see, there are BINs that are higher—in the $189 range—so there is nothing obvious here. There are some no-reserve auctions, so SellerX takes a quick look at completed items, as shown in Figure 5.4.

After analyzing these results, SellerX finds that there is a seller named "bluepro14" who has sold some items for $167. It is hard to tell from completed items if bluepro14 is selling in volume. A useful trick for exploring competition on eBay is to look at an individual seller's selling history. To do this from the eBay home page:

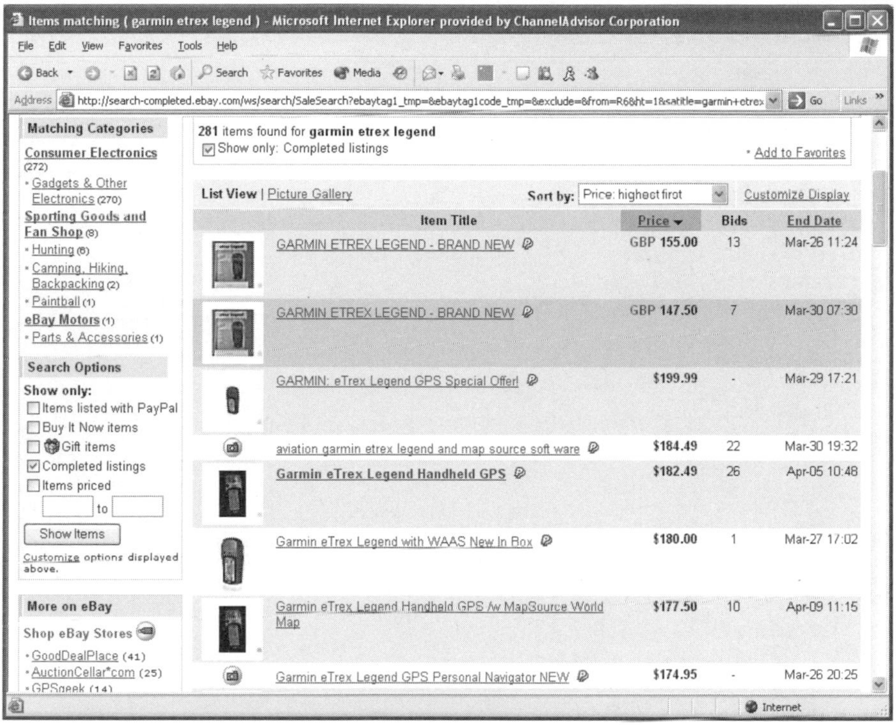

FIGURE 5.4   A look at completed auctions

1. Click on "Search" in the menu bar.

2. Click the "By Seller" tab.

3. Enter the seller's information, as shown in Figure 5.5, being sure to select "All" in the "Include completed items" section.

After exploring bluepro14's statistics, SellerX sees that bluepro14 sold only four eTrex units over the last 30 days and thus is most unlikely to be responsible for such a significant decrease.

Next, SellerX checks Shopping.com, whose results are shown in Figure 5.6.

The price range listed by Shopping.com for the SKU is $158 to $252—the middle point of this is $205, which

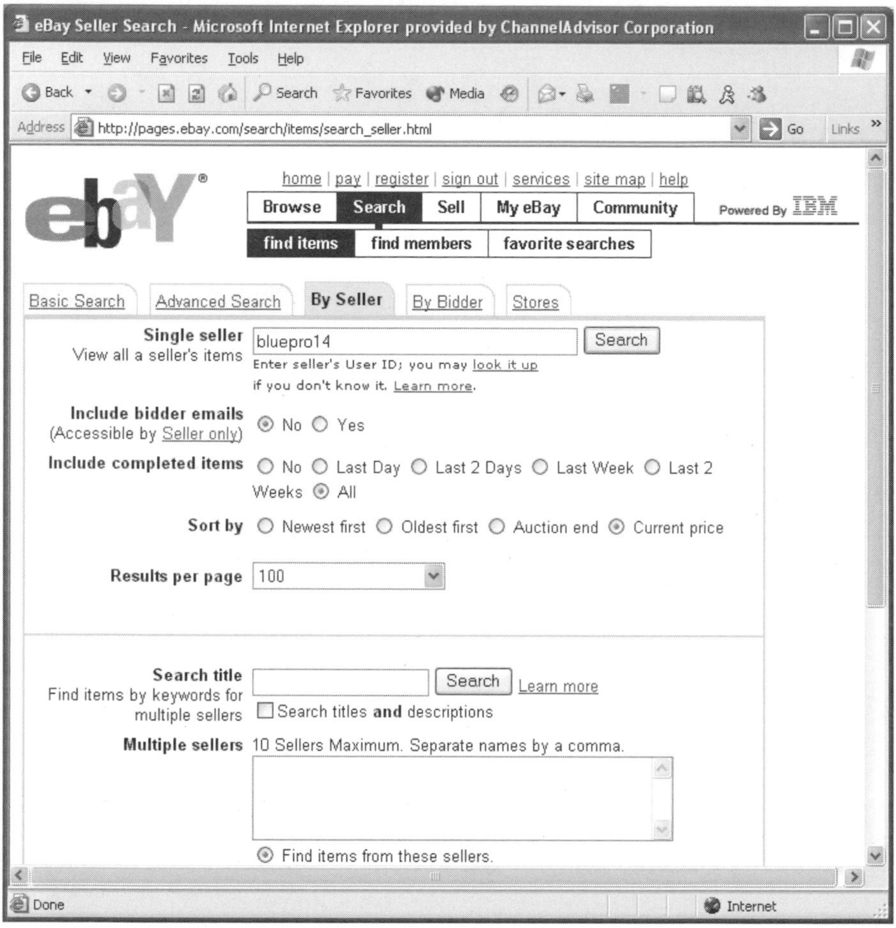

FIGURE 5.5   Viewing an individual seller's sales for the last 30 days

seems reasonable. Also, no name-brand retailers are listed as being lower than $199, which looks good as well. SellerX then checks PriceGrabber.com, PriceSCAN.com, and a number of top retailers.

Next, SellerX checks Amazon.com, as shown in Figure 5.7. As you can see from Figure 5.7, Amazon.com does not list its price for this item, so SellerX logs in and adds it to his Amazon.com shopping cart. Much to SellerX's surprise, after adding the SKU to the shopping cart, he sees that the

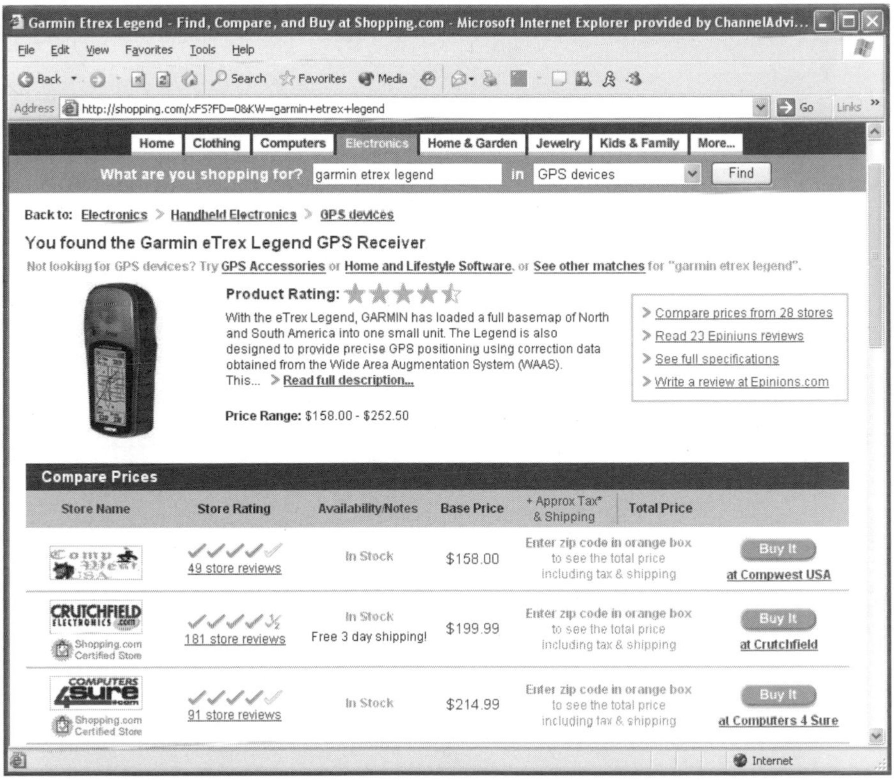

FIGURE 5.6 Shopping.com research for the Garmin eTrex Legend

item is selling at Amazon.com for $164—a significant discount from most eBay sellers, as well as other retailers.

Finally, SellerX goes to the Garmin site, does a search, and quickly learns that Garmin has lowered the price on the model above the Legend and announced another high-end model.

After about 30 minutes of research and armed with knowledge of the product life cycle, SellerX now knows what is going on. Garmin is liquidating the Legend to make room for the new products in the consumer GPS product line. Amazon.com seems to have purchased the end-of-life product in bulk for a significant discount and thus is able to offer it at a lower price than SellerX.

FIGURE 5.7 Amazon.com research for the Garmin eTrex Legend

SellerX's strategy going forward with this knowledge is simple: Sell the current stock for as much as possible (in the $160 to $164 range, to compete with Amazon.com) and do not buy the product anymore for $150, because that price doesn't meet the margin requirement. Also, given the liquidation environment, SellerX has decided that even if he is able to get some more of the product for a discount, it is probably best to wait until the current supply has worked through the system and the ASP stabilizes.

$1NR: An Overused and Potentially Dangerous Strategy

A surprisingly large number of eBay sellers have one pricing strategy: they sell everything in the auction format with no reserve, starting at a dollar ($1NR for short—meaning one dollar, no reserve). The theory goes that by starting at $1.00, buyers will be very attracted to the auction and compete vigorously for the item, thus driving the price to "what the market will bear." It is a common belief among eBay sellers that $1NR yields the highest possible price for an item. Also, $1NR businesses do have the benefit of a very high CR—usually in the range of 90 to 100%—which can mean attractive eBay fees as a percentage of sales, as well.

The problem with the theory is that buyers on eBay are extremely sophisticated, and most utilize the strategy called *sniping*. As you know, on eBay, auctions end at a fixed time. Bidders have found that a very successful strategy is to wait until the last minutes and even seconds of an auction to enter their bid. Sniping is this practice of waiting until the very end of an auction to bid. In fact, there are numerous sophisticated sniping applications that buyers can use to enter their bids. The software does the sniping for them, so they don't have to be online and watch an auction end.

Sniping, plus the hard stop that eBay's auctions have, means that the true market price is frequently not achieved, sophisticated buyers get a deal (by not bidding up an auction in its first six days, the price is relatively low by the end of the auction), but the seller has not achieved market price. The practice of sniping also tends to upset early bidders, who feel cheated when someone swoops in from nowhere in the last seconds to win the item. The sniped bidders frequently would have been willing to pay more for the item, but they don't have time to react to the last-second outbid. Some would argue that eBay's proxy bidding helps defeat outbidding by snipers, but in our experience, buyers are suspicious of the proxy and don't use it as heavily as some might think.

It's also important to understand that eBay is very mainstream now, and not all eBay buyers have time for or enjoy the auction format. Remember that more than 25% of eBay transactions occur through stores or BIN or fixed price sales. There are a large number of "convenience" buyers: they don't want to wait an average of 3.5 days to win an item or put up a fight for an item. With a pure $1NR strategy, you are losing the entire market of convenience buyers.

Also, in a $1NR auction, there is *one* winning bidder, but there may have been five to ten buyers participating in the auction who you would have welcomed at the prices they were willing ultimately to pay. In a pure $1NR strategy business, the theory is that those losing bidders will just move on to the next $1NR auction and contribute to the bidding. Actually, we have found that this is not the case.

How Other Auction Formats Avoid Sniping

If you've ever been to a live auction, you've seen how sniping is avoided: bidding continues until the last bid is placed. There are some non-eBay auction sites that replicate this behavior by having an automatic extension feature. For example, if a bid comes in the last five minutes of an auction, the auction is automatically extended another five minutes to give other bidders a chance to react. This has the benefit of getting close to market price for the seller, but buyers have less of a chance of getting a great deal, and most prefer eBay's format.

Only for the rarest of items do sellers go from one $1NR auction to another, trying continually over the span of weeks to win an item.

Even if you don't believe either of these reasons, we strongly recommend trying to mix in some BIN and fixed-price listings to test if buyers will pay more than what your $1NR auctions are closing for—and to see how many convenience buyers you pick up. You can test by setting your BIN prices to be 5 to 10% higher than the ASP from your $1NR auctions. Our experience is that you'll be pleasantly surprised by the results. Even with a CR in the range of 50 to 60%, your eBay fees will be moderate, and you will actually increase your overall margin.

The $1NR Death Spiral

Now that you understand the dynamics of the price/velocity curve, we will illustrate how a pure $1NR strategy can lead to a death spiral: a rapidly degenerating cycle ultimately resulting in a severe business problem and potentially the death of the business.

SellerX is a jewelry seller with a pure $1NR strategy. SellerX's cost on her largest SKU is $100, and she sells the item for $150. SellerX starts off with GMS of $30,000 per month moving 200 of the SKU a month. SellerX's margin is $50 × 200 = $10,000. SellerX wants to increase the business, so she sells 600 items the next month. This brings GMS of $69,000, but the ASP has decreased to $115, which yields margin of $15 × 600 = $9,000. SellerX is encouraged by the GMS but needs more margin, so she sells 900 items the next month, which further lowers the ASP to the $105 range. Although GMS is $94,500, margin is now at a low of $4,500. In fact, at this point, many $1NR sellers hit cash-flow problems and implode.

In fact, $1NR businesses tend to have a steep chasm in their price/velocity curve, as illustrated in Figure 5.8, compared to the smooth curve shown earlier. Here is the reason why: As the $1NR seller increases listing velocity, more and more buyers (demand) are pulled into the $1NR auctions, soaking up the demand in the marketplace, attracting buyers into auctions that the majority of interested buyers won't win. For example, if you have a ratio of ten bidders per $1NR (and one winner, of course), then you are satisfying one-tenth the demand but tying up the rest. The result is, as you try to scale a $1NR strategy, the ASP hits a plateau and then plummets.

Wouldn't it be better to try to sell to four to eight of the ten bidders?

When Does $1NR Make Sense?

A pure $1NR strategy makes sense in these scenarios:

■ **You have very wide but not deep product selection—for example, if everything you sell is unique.**

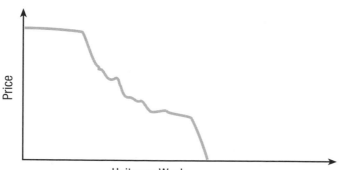

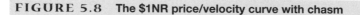

FIGURE 5.8 **The $1NR price/velocity curve with chasm**

- You make more money off shipping than you do on the items you sell. There are many sellers on eBay with very low ASP items that they start for a dollar or even a penny. These sellers are driving transactions so they can make margin on shipping and handling. Note that this is typically not a sustainable business model.

- You view eBay as a promotional vehicle and want to get as many people as possible bidding on your items, regardless of sales.

$1NR is an effective tool that, as you'll see in the next section, can be leveraged with other strategies. However, in a stand-alone, pure form, it is very limited and dangerous.

USE THE PERCEPTION-OF-SCARCITY STRATEGY

5

Remember the example of the seller with the Palms, where he listed 50 of them for sale at a time? Although eBay buyers are frequently considered not very smart, that is a dangerous underestimation. In fact, eBay buyers can smell a deal, and they can also tell when a seller has a lot of inventory and will "wait you out." In the Palm example, imagine you are an eBay buyer. You do a search for a Palm and there are 50 listings, all obviously by the same seller at the same price. Why buy now? Why not watch the seller and see if he will lower prices? The seller obviously has tons of these items, so why not wait?

In fact, you can take a SKU for which you have 1,000 in stock, put it out in a fixed-price listing with quantity 1,000 at a good price, and end up with an unusually low velocity.

The reason is that eBay buyers intuitively understand the laws of supply and demand; they know you have a *lot of* supply, and so they have no reason to buy from you. In fact, it's in their best interest not to buy and actually to wait and see if the price comes down.

The huge mistake in both of these cases is that the seller revealed an important piece of information he should keep confidential: supply.

We've developed a highly effective strategy, called the *perception-of-scarcity strategy,* in which you do not reveal the amount of your inventory (supply). To fully utilize this strategy requires special advanced-scheduling software, but you can still enjoy the benefits if you haven't automated your business.

Getting Started

In the perception-of-scarcity strategy, you run two different types of auction at the same time—together they maximize sales. First, there are two BIN auctions started with a price that is 5 to 10% above the results for a $1NR auction for a SKU. The bulk of the business will be done through the BINs, so they are critical to the strategy.

Second, take 5 to 10% of the amount of inventory you want to move over a given period of time—say, a month—and run $1NR auctions spread strategically over that month. Instead of thinking of these $1NR auctions as "market price," consider them promotional. Before launching the $1NR auctions, insert a link to the BIN auctions and promote them by saying something like: "Don't feel like waiting? Click here to buy this item now!"

Buyer Experience

Now, when the eBay buyer does a search for your item, he or she will be faced with an immediate choice:

1. **Do I get involved in the $1NR auction?**

2. **Or do I buy the BIN? If I do, I need to do it fast, because there's only two.**

This strategy immediately draws convenience buyers to the BIN. Of the buyers who don't choose to BIN and choose to participate in the $1NR, only one will win, leaving the others still wanting the item. Guess what? Many of them will go and grab a BIN as well. Compared to the $1NR strategy where we lose all but one bidder, in this strategy we are capturing potentially all of them.

The key to keeping this strategy going is to keep two BINs live at all times (this is where software comes in handy). It's also important to keep at least one $1NR going to help drive excitement and send losing bidders to the BINs. This is where scheduling software can also come in very handy.

Once you get the handle of this strategy, you can start to experiment with the ratio of $1NR to BINs, as well as the percentage difference between the close of the $1NR and the BIN. For some sellers, we have gotten the spread as high as 20 to 30%, which is more proof that $1NR auctions do not accurately determine market pricing.

Additionally, when you get the strategy going, you can move the BIN up and down and use the results to rapidly determine the price/velocity curve for the SKU.

The beauty of this strategy is that you never reveal the amount of inventory you have, and you use a variety of eBay formats to achieve the goal of maximizing price and velocity.

6 USE THE SECOND-CHANCE-OFFER STRATEGY

In response to troubles sellers have had with buyers not paying (NPBs or deadbeats), eBay recently introduced an interesting feature called Second Chance Offer, or SCO for short.

With an SCO, the seller can offer bidders who did not win the item (also known as underbidders) the opportunity to purchase the item for the amount they bid. Thus, if your highest bidder backs out of the transaction, you can offer the item to the next-highest bidder. Or if you have a reserve auction that does not hit reserve, then you can offer the item to the highest bidder if you decide the bid was close enough.

Although these uses are helpful in various situations, they do not constitute a strategy. The strategy comes into play in the third use of SCO. eBay recently expanded the use of SCO to include offering duplicate items to multiple underbidders. Before we get into the strategy, it's important to understand how this feature works.

An SCO Example

Let's say, for example, you auction an item starting at $50. After 20 bids from 15 bidders, it ends at $100. Table 5.1 shows a list of bids received for this fictitious item.

TABLE 5.1   List of bids placed

BID NUMBER	BIDDER	AMOUNT
1	Bidder1	$51
2	Bidder2	$53
3	Bidder1	$54
4	Bidder3	$55
5	Bidder2	$56
6	Bidder1	$57
7	Bidder3	$65
8	Bidder2	$74
9	Bidder1	$78
10	Bidder4	$85
11	Bidder1	$86
12	Bidder2	$87
13	Bidder3	$90
14	Bidder4	$91
15	Bidder2	$92
16	Bidder4	$93
17	Bidder3	$96
18	Bidder4	$97
19	Bidder1	$98
20	Bidder4	$100

<Auction Closes>

The top bidders' highest bids were:

- **Bidder1**: $98

- **Bidder2**: $92

- **Bidder3**: $96

- **Bidder4**: $100 (winner)

With SCO, you can offer all three underbidders the item at the price they bid. The way this works is that the underbidders receive an SCO e-mail with a link to a special fixed-price listing that is visible only to the underbidder and is available for a limited time. The seller can specify the duration of the SCO, with intervals of one, three, five, or seven days.

So far, the feature looks pretty cool, but the real killer part of the feature is . . . the price! With Second Chance Offers, you pay *no listing fee* (other than the original listing fee and any upgrades for the original listing) and pay only according to the normal final value fee schedule.

Using Second Chance Offer in a Strategy

SCO is a great eBay feature, but it still isn't a strategy. Looking back at the price/velocity curve, here are some facts that drive the SCO strategy:

- Scarcity increases demand and raises bid prices.

- Revealing quantity decreases prices. For example, in a single-unit $1NR auction versus a 100-unit Dutch auction, the $1NR will receive a higher price.

- Dutch auctions are flawed because they reveal how much product is for sale. However, the key problem with Dutch auctions is that the winners all receive the item for the lowest winning bidder's price, which puts significant downward pressure on price. Also, this favors the buyer but not the seller. To favor the seller, eBay would have each buyer pay the amount he or she bid, because that's what the buyer was willing to pay for the item.

The SCO strategy, like the perception-of-scarcity strategy, does not have any of these problems and thus can simultaneously optimize price and velocity. Here's how it works. Let's say you have deep quantity of a certain SKU. First, you run one and only one auction-style listing, with no BIN and no reserve (we'll cover the starting price shortly). Bidders bid up the auction, and it closes with a winning bidder. Then you use SCO to offer the item to any bidders who placed bids that match your margin target. As you get the hang of the strategy, you can start to experiment with more listings, moving the margin target and altering the starting price.

There are two different flavors of the SCO strategy; which one you choose depends on your tolerance for risk. The less-risky strategy starts the auction bidding at the price where you hit your margin target, and then at auction close, you offer SCOs to every bidder.

The second approach starts the auction at $1.00 and then offers SCOs to bidders who happen to be over the margin target price.

The benefit of the "start at margin" flavor is you are guaranteed that every bidder will be over your margin target, and you also "weed out" bidders who may be looking for a very low price. However, there will be fewer total bidders. Thus, the conversion rate of SCO underbidders will be very high.

With the "start at $1.00" flavor, the auction will tend to have more bidders and a potentially higher closing price. The only negative is that the auction could close below your target margin price. Also, we have seen that if the auction does close above your margin target, with the $1.00 starting price, SCO underbidders are less likely to convert than with the "start at margin" approach.

Why Is the SCO Strategy So Beneficial?

The SCO strategy has significant benefits:

- You can actively manage the price for which you sell your items.

- The seller does not reveal the quantity for sale to the buyer, thus creating a perception of scarcity and a call to action.

- There is little or no risk. Risk can be managed by alternating between the $1NR start or the "start at margin" approach.

- Because of the absence of additional listing fees, this strategy will generate the lowest eBay fees as a percentage of sales.

- To really "juice" this strategy, you can leverage some of the promotional strategies from the next chapter that wouldn't be economical on a single listing, but when allocated across many SCO items, they increase the return on investment.

- Unlike a Dutch auction, where each winning bidder "wins" for the lowest winning bidder's price, with SCO, bidders pay what they previously bid, which is what they were willing to pay and not a "steal."

- You can manage your sales based on margin by SKU. For one SKU, you may be at your target selling the item for more than $18. For another, the target may be $29. With the SCO strategy, you can decide SKU by SKU where you want to draw the line on which underbidders are extended offers.

- Snipers are welcome. With the SCO strategy, you actually welcome snipers. They increase the number of SCO offers and drive up the price at the end of the auction.

- With advanced auction-management software, you can completely automate the strategy and even use formulas. For example, you can set up the strategy, by SKU, to automatically extend SCOs to underbidders for the SKU cost plus the margin target percentage.

The SCO Strategy vs. the Perception-of-Scarcity Strategy

In this chapter, we have introduced two advanced strategies that can completely change the way you think about eBay. The key to picking the pricing strategy that's right for you is to try each and measure their results.

There's also no reason you can't mix the two strategies. You may have one class of inventory that does better with the SCO strategy and another that is maximized by the perception-of-scarcity strategy.

Typically, the SCO strategy works best for products that sell in the range of 100 to 200 units per month. The perception-of-scarcity strategy plus some promotional push can be effective for the products in the range of 150 to 500 units per month.

In all cases, however, SCO has more margin control and higher margins generally, because of the lower eBay fees.

Price and Classifications

In Chapter 4, "Product," we discussed dividing your SKU base into three classes of product. Using this same principle, you can use the classifications to determine how to price the various SKUs.

Class A Product

As previously mentioned, Class A product is recently acquired product on which you need to make margin. Given this constraint, you're going to want to be in the highest-margin portion of the price/velocity curve, which is typically the portion on the left of the curve.

Therefore, the eBay pricing strategy for Class A product is fixed-price/BIN at the target price/margin levels, potentially with a small percentage of no-reserve auctions linked to the BIN listings to drive excitement and attract buyers. As a sanity check, you should keep the BINs at 10% or higher above the no-reserve auction closing prices, to drive convenience purchases.

Class B Product

Class B product is product that has been on hand for a while, and you need to move it rapidly or risk not making margin on it. In this case, you want to be farther on the right of the price/velocity curve—turning up the velocity and sacrificing some of the price.

The eBay strategy for this class of product may be similar to that of Class A, but with a higher percentage of no-reserve auctions. You may also come off the BIN price by 5 to 10%, and make sure you have one of the most competitive BIN prices and are pricing your BINs at no more than 5% above the average no-reserve auction closing price.

It also may make sense to run some Dutch auctions with quantities in the range of 5 to 10% of your inventory. As you'll see in the next chapter, you may also want to consider some special promotions to accelerate the sales of these items.

Class C Product

If you'll recall, Class C product is liquidation product that favors velocity over price/yield. Class C product needs to be sold rapidly, so consider a large Dutch auction with heavy promotion or potentially no-reserve auctions. As you'll see in the next chapter, although you may take a loss on Class C product, there are promotional techniques you can use to maximize the promotional benefit of a great deal for your Class A and B stock.

Case Study

DesignerAthletic

Seller: designerathletic (7284 ⭐) 🏆Power Seller me ⊜

DesignerAthletic has been on eBay for less than a year, in the shoe category. In that short amount of time, by leveraging very advanced pricing strategies, DesignerAthletic has become one of the top sellers in the category, quickly surpassing sellers with tens of thousands more feedback points and many more years of experience.

eBay Vitals

- **GMS**: $200,000–$300,000 per month
- **ASP**: $40–$60
- **CR**: 40–50%
- **Feedback**: 99.5%

Background

In 2003, the folks at DesignerAthletic had an idea to leverage eBay to sell excess athletic shoes for retailers. They figured that instead of severely discounting 100 size-seven Nikes in a physical store, where only one person with a size-seven foot may come in per day, why not put that inventory on eBay, where they could have hundreds, if not thousands, of size-seven people searching for a great deal on shoes.

Based in North Carolina, DesignerAthletic has six staff members. They process two tractor-trailer trucks of shoes per business day.

Figure 5.9 shows DesignerAthletic's About Me page. Notice that there are many ways for potential buyers to shop: by brand, size, gender, and so on, and some special offers are highlighted on the About Me page.

Figure 5.10 shows one of DesignerAthletic's live items for sale. Highlights include the quality of the image, the easy links for shopping by gender/size, and finally the suggested retail price.

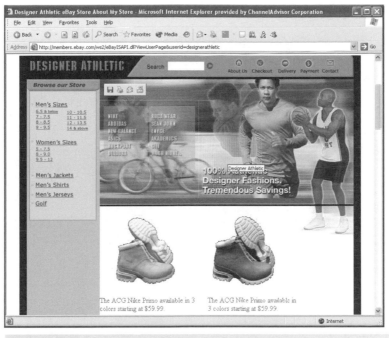

FIGURE 5.9   DesignerAthletic's About Me page

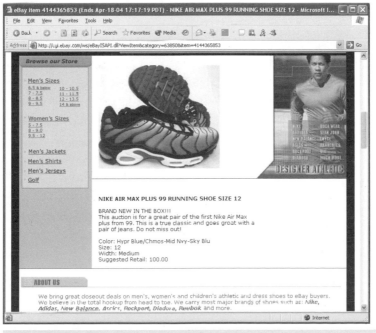

FIGURE 5.10   A DesignerAthletic item for sale

DesignerAthletic and Price

DesignerAthletic experimented with every possible pricing strategy on eBay: pure $1NR, pure BIN/fixed price, Dutch auctions, hybrid approaches, the perception of scarcity, and so on. After trying all those approaches, they have come up with the following pricing strategy, which has dramatically accelerated their business:

- They start every shoe with no reserve at a formula-based starting price, based on the average market price and their margin targets.

- The starting price achieves their margin target, but because it is usually such a great deal, the price is bid up significantly.

- If they have the depth of the SKU, DesignerAthletic employs the SCO strategy, offering SCOs to all underbidders.

- Each SCO bid-up not only accelerates velocity, but also expands margin.

- If they have hundreds of an item, they will run some BINs and some $1NR auctions in a kind of perception-of-scarcity strategy, to really ramp up the volume.

Figure 5.11 shows a great example of this strategy in action. In this example, a $130 retail-priced pair of shoes were auctioned with no reserve at a great starting price of $89.99. Note that this price is 30% off retail—right in the eBay buyer sweet spot and an awesome deal sure to draw in bidders. For argument's sake, let's say that DesignerAthletic's margin target is 15%. Thus, their cost would be around $78.

Four bidders fought it out and drove the price to $103.50. Again, for argument's sake, Table 5.2 shows some sample SCOs that would have been sent out, with margin for each.

Although they would have been at target margin to sell the SKU with one bid at $89.99, DesignerAthletic's clever use of the SCO strategy has resulted in a near-doubling of the margin target!

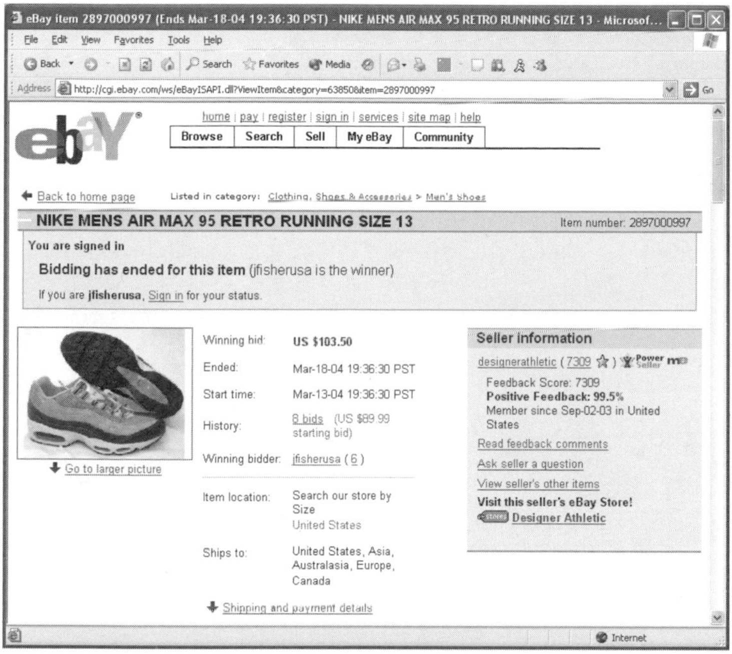

FIGURE 5.11 An example of DesignerAthletic's pricing strategy

What's more, the eBay fees saved are significant. Let's look at the eBay fees under the SCO strategy and then compare them to the eBay fees without using SCO.

Table 5.3 shows the eBay fees with SCO.

Table 5.4 shows the eBay fees without SCO (assuming four listings, all starting at $09.99). In this non-SCO scenario, eBay fees are 5.75% of sales.

TABLE 5.2 Sample SCOs and margins

BUYER	PRICE PAID	MARGIN MADE	MARGIN %
Underbidder1	$98.00	$20.00	26%
Underbidder2	$100.00	$22.00	28%
Underbidder3	$101.00	$23.00	29%
Winner	$103.50	$25.50	33%
Total	$402.50	$90.50	29%

TABLE 5.3   Sample eBay fees for SCOs

BUYER	PRICE PAID	EBAY FEES	NOTES
Underbidder1	$98.00	$1.31 + (2.75% × $73) = $3.32	No listing fee
Underbidder2	$100.00	$1.31 + (2.75% × $75) = $3.37	No listing fee
Underbidder3	$101.00	$1.31 + (2.75% × $76) = $3.40	No listing fee
Winner	$103.50	$2.40 + $1.31 + (2.75% × $78.50) = $5.87	Listing fee
Total	$402.50	$15.96	3.96%

TABLE 5.4   Sample eBay fees without SCOs

BUYER	PRICE PAID	EBAY FEES
Underbidder1	$98.00	$2.40 + $1.31 + (2.75% × $73) = $5.72
Underbidder2	$100.00	$2.40 + $1.31 + (2.75% × $75) = $5.77
Underbidder3	$101.00	$2.40 + $1.31 + (2.75% × $76) = $5.80
Winner	$103.50	$2.40 + $1.31 + (2.75% × $78.50) = $5.87
Total	$402.50	$23.16

By using the SCO strategy, not only is the velocity increased, but also there is a savings difference of 1.8%, which drops straight to the bottom line!

DesignerAthletic experimented with the SCO strategy starting with $1NR, but they settled on the higher bid price for two main reasons:

- It decreases the amount of inbound pre-sales customer support e-mails. Lots of buyers are "window shoppers" who may bid early, at very low prices, but do not participate when the auction gets in the range of $50 and up. Though the window shoppers do drive up the price, DesignerAthletic found the extra support they generated was not worth the potential for a higher ASP.

- There is considerable risk that items will sell for below the margin target price.

Other Strategies of Interest

DesignerAthletic invests heavily in what they call "honest listing." Unlike many sellers, who have minimal descriptions, fuzzy shipping costs, and poor-quality images, DesignerAthletic works hard to make sure every product's description completely captures the product and that all terms and conditions are crisply presented.

Chapter 5 Summary

Sniping—Sniping occurs when a buyer places a winning bid in the last minutes or seconds of an auction. Smart eBay buyers almost exclusively use sniping as a buying strategy, and numerous applications for automating sniping are available.

Price/velocity curve—The price/velocity curve shows the relationship between the price you achieve for your goods and the volume you are able to sell over an amount of time. Our discussion of the price/velocity curve assumes that demand is constant and only supply is varied. As volume, or velocity, increases, prices tend to come down. Alternatively, you can achieve higher prices by decreasing the velocity.

Second Chance Offer (SCO)—SCO is a feature that allows a seller to make offers to underbidders for the amount they bid on an item. Typically used for reserve auctions and NPB situations, it can also be used to accelerate velocity as the foundation of a pricing strategy.

KEY CONCEPTS

In this chapter, we discussed the second *P* of the Five P's framework: price. The most important concept related to price is the price/velocity curve and how it can affect your business. Once you understand the relationship between price and velocity for your eBay business, you will be able to make smarter buying decisions and start developing interesting new selling strategies.

One overused and dangerous strategy is the pure one-dollar start, no reserve auction (also known as $1NR) utilized by many sellers. Once you understand the price/velocity curve, you will see that the $1NR strategy causes the price to drop rapidly as velocity increases. Actually, the $1NR strategy accelerates the price decrease, because much of the demand is captured in $1NR auctions rather than being converted into buyers. This effect creates a chasm, or large dip, in the price/velocity curve. Contrary to popular opinion, due to

Chapter 5 Summary

sniping, $1NR auctions do not typically achieve true market price. Also, $1NR auctions do not appeal to the convenience buyer or the buyer who doesn't feel comfortable with the auction format. Alternative basic strategies can be utilized, such as increasing the mix of BINs, reserve auctions, fixed-price listings, and starting auctions at a higher price, closer to the desired price, rather than starting at $1.00.

Two proven, cutting-edge strategies were introduced. The first, called the "perception-of-scarcity strategy," leverages the positives of the $1NR auction, but as a promotional draw. BIN auctions concurrently draw both the convenience buyer and the losing $1NR bidders into buying your products.

The second strategy, based on the Second Chance Offer eBay feature, allows you to start a no-reserve auction and then offer underbidders more quantities of the same items at the price they bid (their maximum), and you can choose the margin target. With the SCO strategy, there are two options for starting things. You can choose to start the auctions at a minimum margin target, so that you are guaranteed all SCOs are above your ASP/margin target. The second option starts the auctions at $1.00 with no reserve, which tends to increase the winning bidder amount but increases the risk of an auction closing below your margin targets.

Finally, we revisited the concept of classifications first introduced in Chapter 4, and we provided appropriate pricings based on the three classifications.

EXERCISES

1. Take your most popular SKU and, over the course of four weeks, determine the price/velocity curve for the product.

Chapter 5 Summary

2. Try taking two SKUs that are similar. Run one for a month with a pure $1NR strategy and another with the perception-of-scarcity strategy. Which strategy was most effective?

3. Next, try the same SKU and utilize the SCO strategy. Now which is most effective?

4. The next time you source product, try to negotiate a volume discount, but make sure you do so with a clear understanding of the price/velocity curve for the product.

SIX

Promotion

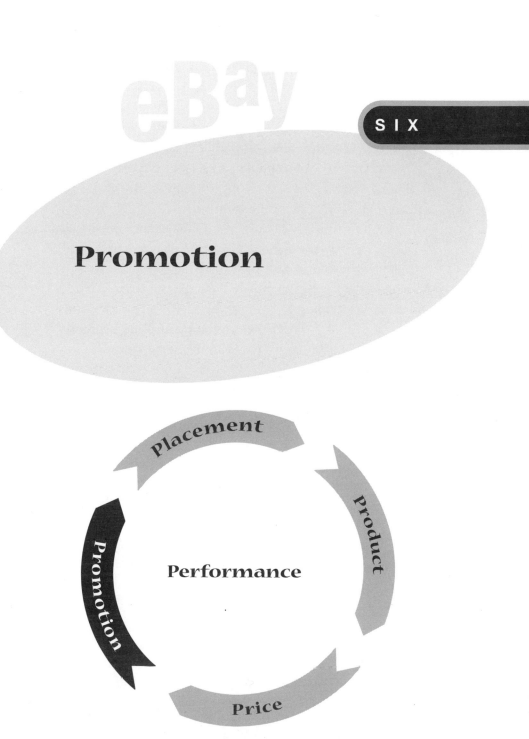

The third P in the strategic eBay framework: promotion

he third *P* of the Five P's strategic framework is *promotion*. Without promotion, the best product and pricing strategies won't increase your business, because promotion is what draws buyers to your items. Many sellers are familiar with the basic options available for promotion, but very few utilize them.

Interestingly, when you look at the state of the art of Internet marketing, most eBay sellers are comparatively in the Stone Age. For example, a top retail Web site operator knows everything about its buyers, such as how buyers find its store, where they come from, where they go when they leave, how much time they spend online, and much more. Unfortunately, the state of the art on eBay is a basic traffic counter that shows only how many unique visitors an auction has had—and potentially the timing of those visitors.

In this chapter, we work to bring you up to speed with the rest of the world. Before long, you'll be promoting your eBay business on a par with the best e-tailers.

Promotion and the Price/Velocity Curve

Before you consider specific promotional ideas, you need to understand the importance of promotion to your eBay business: promotion is key to your success. Figure 6.1 illustrates just how powerful strong promotion can be.

Figure 6.1 shows the price/velocity curve that you're familiar with from the last chapter. However, notice the significant addition of the promotional dotted line, which actually extends the price/velocity curve. As this graphic indicates, a strong promotional strategy can dramatically increase the velocity at which you sell items, but without the price degradation we discussed in the previous chapter.

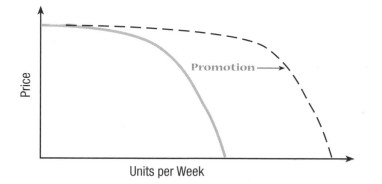

FIGURE 6.1 **The price/velocity curve with promotion**

How is this possible? Basically, as you'll recall, the discussion of the price/velocity curve assumed that demand was *constant*. Promotional activity extends the price/velocity curve by adding new demand to the mix. With the addition of new demand, more buyers are available to buy your items. Thus, you can increase the number of units sold over a specific amount of time.

Remember the perception-of-scarcity strategy? The $1NR auctions were considered promotional, used primarily to attract more buyers into the equation, rather than to sell a significant number of items.

In the rest of this chapter, we cover the top promotional tools at your disposal and detail how to get the most leverage out of them. Once you implement these promotional strategies, not only should you see a boost in your current sales, but you should also be able to scale your eBay business much more rapidly than before.

7 OPTIMIZE YOUR EBAY SEARCH RESULTS

The single most significant promotional tool at your disposal is the eBay search engine. More than 80 million searches a day are performed through the eBay search engine, by buyers who are looking to purchase the items they seek.

In fact, if you follow broader Internet trends, the big discovery in the last two years is the results Internet marketers achieve when advertising with search engines such as Overture/Yahoo! and Google. Search generates the best results because of two ingredients:

1. **The searcher has told you exactly what he or she is looking for.**

2. **If the search is commercial in nature (which all are at eBay), then the searcher is typically close to buying.**

Thus, search traffic tends to "convert" at a much higher rate than any other form of Internet advertising, such as banner ads.

These same rules of thumb for Internet marketing in general definitely apply to eBay in particular; in some cases, they apply even more strongly to eBay than to the rest of the Internet. One of the best things about eBay is that there are really only two kinds of users: buyers and sellers. Nobody goes to eBay to check a stock quote or read the latest news; people are there to buy or sell—period.

Understanding eBay Buyer Search Behavior

Before we look at optimizing your listings for eBay's search, it's important to understand more about the behavior of eBay searchers. Our data indicates that 80% of eBay buyers use the search engine to locate the items they are looking for; approximately 20% are just browsing (more on browsing later). Of the 80% who use the search engine, the majority (about 70%) use only "Search title" versus "Search title and description."

Given these dynamics, for every 100 searches, 70 are title only and 30 are for title and description.

This mix, plus the fact that search is the preferred buyer mechanism for finding things, means that the auction title is the single most important promotional tool at your disposal.

Title Is King

eBay recently expanded the maximum length of auction titles from 45 to 55 characters. Deciding what fills those 55 characters is one of the most important promotional decisions you make, so it must be done as intelligently as possible. Since you are given 55 characters in the title, the best rule of thumb is to use every character you are given.

It's important to know the top searches for your category, so

> **N O T E**
> eBay Store listings are displayed only if the main eBay search engine returns ten or fewer results, which is rarely the case. Therefore, if you plan on using eBay Store listings, you will need to promote them by sending traffic from your auction and fixed-price listings that are in the search engine.

that you can know not only "what's hot," but also what search terms buyers are using, so you can target them in your titles and generate the most traffic.

There are a couple of places where you can find this information. First, eBay has an area called Seller Central: http://www.ebay.com/sellercentral. Within Seller Central, you will find an area called "Sell by Category." There you can find "What's Hot" and "In Demand" areas for each category.

Figure 6.2 shows an example for the Entertainment category, which displays the top ten searches for the category. Each category is different, and some provide much more information than others do. For example, the toy category

FIGURE 6.2   Top searches for the eBay entertainment category

provides the top ten searches for all the subcategories as well as for the entire toy category.

Also, from the eBay home page, if you click into a category, you land on that category's portal page. Usually on this page, top searches are listed for the convenience of buyers, but they are also useful for sellers.

Figure 6.3 shows the top search area of the Entertainment category's landing page.

Armed with this detailed information on buyers' search behavior, you can begin optimizing your auction titles. Following are some examples of good titles and bad titles.

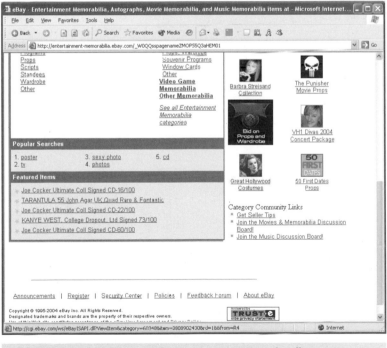

FIGURE 6.3 The search area on a category landing page

How Buyers Really Search

Contrary to popular opinion, our research has shown that most buyers do not search on eBay slang, such as "NIB" (new in box), "NWT" (new with tag), or "NR" (no reserve). Instead, most buyers search on:

- Brand names
- Model numbers
- General descriptions
- Condition

In fact, eBay is rapidly implementing "item specifics" that require the seller to select the brand, model, condition, size, color, and so on of items when listing. Then buyers can search on these specific attributes. This policy will clear the way for the 55-character title to be 100% description, and not poorly defined eBay slang.

BAD TITLES

- "sony dvd player"
  This title is too short (it's only 15 characters) and not specific enough.

- "bruce springsteen CD"
  No specifics on album title or other points of interest to buyers. Also too short (20 characters).

- "Ralph Lauren shirt—NWT NR!!"
  This title is short (29 characters) and uses abbreviations familiar only to a few eBay buyers.

- **"$$$LOOK$$$ awesome new digital camera"**
  Buyers do not search on "$$$LOOK$$$," and the title tells us nothing about the camera (37 characters).

GREAT TITLES

- **"Kenmore 30" Gas Self-Clean Freestanding Range White"**
  The title has 50 characters, it's very descriptive, and it has lots of keywords.

- **"Rio 128MB Portable Digital MP3 Player w/FM model: S35S"**
  This 54-character title includes the model number and many top keywords.

- **"Sony PEG-TJ25 CLIÉ Color Personal Organizer PDA NEW"**
  This very descriptive title consists of 51 characters, includes the model number, and covers the top search terms.

- **"Grand Theft Auto: Vice City (PlayStation 2) FREE SHIP"**
  This title has 53 characters, is descriptive, and includes an eye catcher, "FREE SHIP."

Some advanced auction-management systems offer technology that will actually let you see what users have been searching on to find your items. This technology gives you important data you can use to run tests and better learn what eBay buyers are searching on.

When testing, you can use this functionality to post two auctions with different titles and definitively measure the traffic to each (and the search terms), so you can pick the title or title elements that generated the most traffic to your item.

Figure 6.4 shows a sample report of top searches for an item.

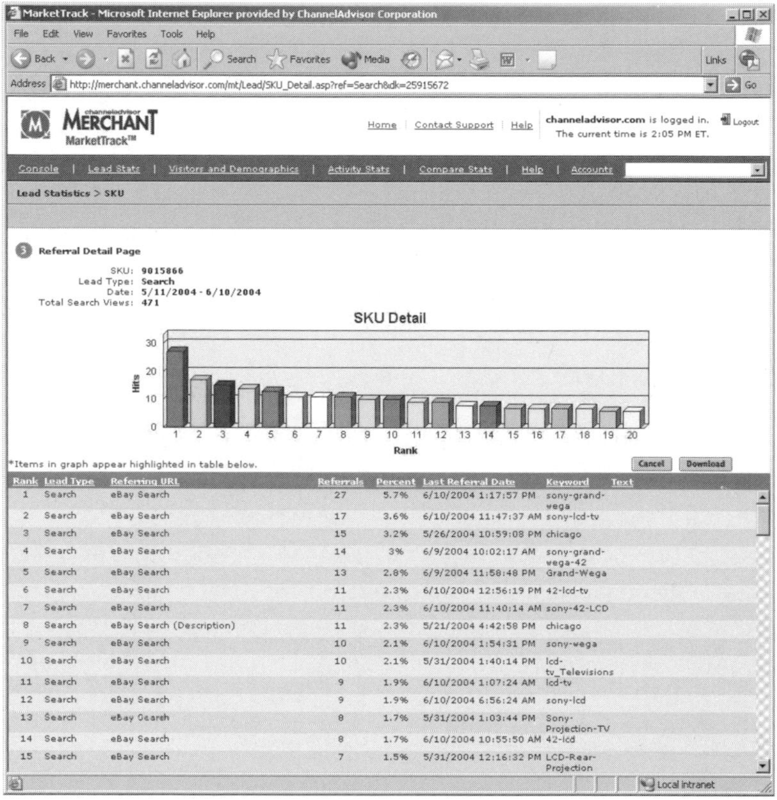

FIGURE 6.4   Sample report of top searches

Subtitles

eBay recently introduced a new feature called Subtitle. For $0.50 per listing fee, you can now place additional text (55 characters, to be exact) in your listing's search results, as an "eye catcher." Note that the eBay search engine does *not* index subtitles, and therefore keywords in subtitles do not affect search results. For example, consider the following title and subtitle combination:

Title: Garmin GPS 8mb like new—great price LOOK!! LOOK!!

Subtitle: This Garmin eTrex Legend features automated map

If users search on "eTrex" or "garmin etrex legend" using the "title only" search on eBay's front page or under "Search," your item will *not* show up in the eBay search results, because the subtitle is not included in title-only searches.

Figure 6.5 shows the results for a search "beanie baby," where the first item shows subtitles in action. The subtitle is "87 bears 17 cats and over 35 dogs and much more."

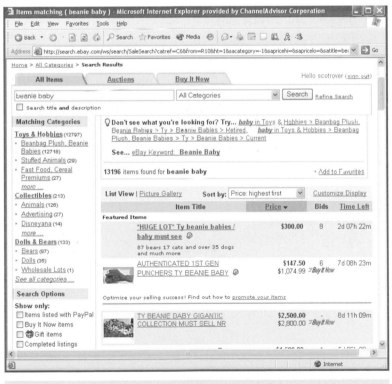

FIGURE 6.5 An example of the Subtitle feature in the first listing

Given the fact that this listing upgrade really doesn't drive more traffic except by "getting attention" in the listings, we typically do not recommend it. For some situations, say, if the item you are selling is relatively expensive (more than $200) and the search results are *very* competitive for the most popular terms (over 1,000), then the Subtitle feature can be a good investment. For expensive items, if Subtitle drives just one or two buyers to look at and bid on your item, it will more than pay for itself.

Unfortunately, there is no way to measure the effectiveness of Subtitle unless you run a scientific study. You would have to list two of the exact same item—one with and one without a subtitle—at different times, but with everything else the same, to see which one got the most traffic.

We have performed this test numerous times and have not found a consistent, measurable difference from using Subtitle. However, many eBay buyers do say that sellers who use Subtitle to point out the "extras" available with an item do draw their attention more than those listings without subtitles. So, the jury is still out on whether the extra attention is worth the $0.50. We leave it to you to draw your own conclusions.

Featured Listings and Other Upgrades

eBay offers a dizzying array of listing upgrades that, like Subtitle, are geared toward increasing attention to your items when eBay buyers are searching. The listing upgrades do not affect whether or not your item will appear in the search results. Instead, they dictate how the listing looks. In the case of the "Featured Plus!" upgrade, your item shows up higher in the results. Note that prices on these options change on a very regular basis, so check eBay directly for the latest fees.

- **Home Page Featured ($39.95/$79.95). With the Home Page Featured upgrade, your item will show up as one of the six listings on eBay's home page under "Featured Items." Given the price of this upgrade, the best way to get any return on investment is to have the link go to either a very large quantity Dutch/fixed-price listing or to a listing placed using the perception-of-scarcity strategy. In the latter case, you would send the traffic to an auction and quickly then take buyers to a large-quantity, fixed-price listing.**

  Home Page Featured seems to be very effective at selling diet pills and items valued more than $500, from diamond rings to airplanes. We do not recommend Home Page Featured except in the most special of circumstances.

- **Featured Plus! ($19.95). This upgrade used to be a very good investment: if you had 5 to 30 of something, you could feature a Dutch auction and see stellar results. Unfortunately, eBay changed the functionality, and the results haven't added up since. Before the change, Featured Plus! made your item show up in the "Featured" section on the top of the first search results page, regardless of closing time.**

  Featured Plus! items now show up on the top of whatever search results page they would normally appear on. For example, if you have an item running in a seven-day auction and there are 1,000 search results, your Featured Plus! item will not show up on the top of the first search results page until the last day of the auction. Even then, it may show up for only part of the last day. Why the last day? The updated Featured Plus! system chooses the page on which the featured item

appears based on the item's closing time. Therefore, your item typically shows up on the front page in the featured area only if it is closing in 1 to 24 hours (depending on the total number of items in the search results).

eBay made this change because for some searches, there were so many featured items that they filled the first several pages of search results. Although the new system is less cluttered for those popular terms, it has significantly decreased the value of this option.

We typically recommend Featured Plus! only if you have very good traffic data and are able to time the promotion to be prominent at peak traffic time for the item you are selling. Also, to make the economics work better on a per-item basis, it makes sense to send the traffic either to a Dutch auction or to a multi-quantity, fixed-price listing.

- **Gallery Featured ($19.95).** This upgrade causes your item to show up in the top of the "Picture Gallery" in a special featured section. Our research indicates that most eBay buyers do not visit the gallery; therefore, we have never recommended this particular listing upgrade.

- **Highlight ($5.00).** Like Subtitle, Highlight is an attention getter or eye catcher. Highlight displays your item with a colorful background in the search results, rather than a white background. As eye-catching options go, this is the most expensive, and unless you have a very competitive landscape for a high-ASP item, Highlight is not worth the expense.

- **Bold ($1.00).** Bold is another attention getter, and although the cost is more reasonable, it's still not very effective for day-to-day items.

- **Gift Services ($0.25).** Selecting the Gift Services icon places a little picture of a present by your listing in search and browse results. This is usually meant to indicate that either you think the item would make a great gift or you are willing to ship to a third party, provide gift wrapping, and so on. This feature generally makes sense only during the holidays—and only if you plan to offer some of the services mentioned.

- **Gallery ($0.25).** Gallery does three things for you. First, it shows a thumbnail in the search results—so it's another attention getter. Second, the thumbnail also shows up when buyers browse eBay. Finally, with Gallery your image shows up in the eBay Picture Gallery.

   Our research indicates that although Gallery is the least expensive of the attention-getting options, it is by far the most effective. When running two listings that were identical except that one utilized Gallery and the other didn't, the results are measurable. In fact, we recommend Gallery for any item that is more than $10 and not a "commodity" item. For example, it probably does not make sense to buy Gallery for a *Finding Nemo* DVD.

Given all of the listing upgrades, our research still indicates that the best thing you can do to promote your items is to spend your time optimizing and enhancing the 55-character title. Once you feel you have a 100% perfect title, then Gallery and Subtitle are potentially economical options that you can test and then see the results.

Expensive options such as Featured Plus!, Highlight, and Bold should be used for only the most special of items. If you do choose to use one of these upgrades, make sure to have the traffic from the promotion go to a multi-item listing or to a listing that leverages the traffic for other sales.

A Word about ROI

When Internet marketers look at spending extra for promotional activities, they are quick to calculate ROI, or return on investment. In other words, if you spent $10 on promotions, did you make your $10 back? If so, what was the return on that investment? For example, if you spend $1,000 on promotions and it drives additional sales of $10,000, the ROI on that investment is 10. Your investment returned ten times the amount spent on the promotion.

Unfortunately, calculating the ROI of many of the paid promotional activities on eBay is nearly impossible because of the following:

■ **How do you calculate the value of a bidder or a bid? In e-commerce, it's clear when someone comes to your site and buys something (converts). On eBay, you may spend money on a promotion for a bidder who bids but doesn't win. There's definitely a value there, but it's not as easy to calculate and understand as in basic e-commerce.**

■ **eBay hosts the pages for bidding and buying, and it doesn't reveal where the user came from or provide ROI calculations. Therefore, as an eBay seller, the only real data you have to help see an ROI picture is traffic. Not all traffic is created equal, and if you can't tell which traffic converted at what rate, traffic-based ROI, although it's intuitively useful, doesn't give a real picture of what's going on.**

For example, the only way to try to figure out the ROI on a promotional feature, say the Bold listing enhancement, is to run a "blind test," in which you list one item without the feature and one with and compare the results. Unfortunately, this isn't always as scientific as we would like, because any number of changes can cause different results. For example, what if a new competitor comes into the market after you have done the first test?

Hopefully, eBay will eventually provide sellers more ROI data as they become more sophisticated. Until that time, ROI calculations for eBay promotional items will remain somewhat in the Stone Age.

Timing Is Everything

Besides optimizing your title, the second most important thing you can do promotionally is to time your auction closings very carefully. Because we know that 80% of the buyers use the search engine and that by default the search results are sorted by end time (soonest to latest), timing your auctions to close during peak search times will *significantly* improve traffic to your auctions, resulting in more bids. Best of all, timing your auctions is free, unless you choose to use the eBay scheduling feature, for $0.10 per listing.

Generally, the peak traffic times are in the evenings, from 8:00 to 12:00 Eastern time, with weekends generally showing more activity than weekdays. Although these times are broadly the peak traffic times, we encourage you to at least use counters or more sophisticated analysis software to give you detailed analytics for each SKU's peak traffic times and then optimize toward those times.

It's important to realize that peak traffic times can actually change throughout the year. For example, starting after Thanksgiving every year, we have seen an additional busy time for most categories from noon to 3:00 p.m. Eastern time, which is driven by "at work" shoppers using their lunch hour to shop on eBay.

eBay Keywords

As previously mentioned, one of the most effective marketing devices on the broader Internet is paid search via Over-
ture/Yahoo! and Google. eBay has taken a page from these
companies' books and recently introduced a similar program *within* eBay, called eBay Keywords. eBay Keywords
gives sellers the opportunity to bid on specific eBay search
terms. If you are willing to pay more than anyone else, you
can have a banner ad show up prominently on the search results page. Figure 6.6 shows a sample search for "dvd player"
and the eBay Keywords banner associated with that search.

FIGURE 6.6   An eBay Keywords search on "dvd player"

An eBay partner, adMarketplace, powers the eBay Keywords program, so do not be alarmed if you click on the eBay Keywords link and find that you have been redirected to the admarketplace.net Web site.

In the example shown in Figure 6.6, the seller "ac-trust" has effectively used the eBay Keywords promotional tool to draw significant attention to his store over all the 64,000 other listing results.

How eBay Keywords Works

Like the larger, paid search engines on the Internet, Google and Overture/Yahoo!, eBay Keywords basically auctions the banner ad position shown in Figure 6.6, awarding the spot to the seller willing to pay the most per clickthrough on the banner advertisement.

> **N O T E**
> In the eBay Keywords program, the amount you are willing to pay per click is called the "cost per click," or CPC.

Once your search is set up, if you have the highest CPC, when a buyer does a search on your chosen keywords, your banner will be presented. eBay Keywords then shows the ads for the buyer based on a "frequency-capping" algorithm. Basically, the highest CPC ad is shown to the buyer for the first three searches, then the second-highest CPC ad is shown for the fourth through the sixth search, the third-highest is shown for the seventh through the ninth search, and so on.

This may sound unusual, but many buyers do page through five to ten pages of results, so most likely the top three banner ads will be shown.

Performance-Based Marketing

The beauty of the eBay Keywords program is that you pay only when a potential buyer clicks on the banner ad. Commonly referred to as *performance-based marketing* in the broader Internet world, the "pay-per-click" model can have a very high ROI. If you compare this type of program to one that isn't tied to performance, you can see why. For example, consider eBay's Highlight feature, where you pay $5 for a listing enhancement but never know how much extra traffic or attention that $5 generated. eBay Keywords allows you to take the same $5 and allocate it to the same item you would have used the Highlight listing enhancement for, but now you will know exactly how many clicks go to the item. Also, you can calculate how much you want to pay per click.

Unfortunately, at the time of this writing, eBay Keywords stops at the click level. In other words, you don't know which of the clicks converts into bidders/buyers, so you can't calculate a "click to purchase/bid" ROI model. However, even given this current limitation, the program should be considered by all sellers, because it is much more economical and performance driven than any other eBay promotional program.

A useful side benefit of working with the eBay Keywords program is that it gives you experience with this form of promotion. Down the road, if you decide to expand beyond eBay, you will be prepared to use search engines such as Google and Overture/Yahoo! to promote your non-eBay activities. eBay Keywords allows you to experiment in a much safer and controlled (and less expensive) program than the broader Internet search engines.

Details about how the program works can be found at:
http://ebay.admarketplace.net/ebay/resources/faqs.html

Getting Started with eBay Keywords

Designed to be a powerful performance-based system, the eBay Keywords program can be somewhat intimidating for eBay businesspeople who may not be familiar with this form of Internet marketing. As mentioned, however, we have found that eBay Keywords is one of the highest-ROI promotional opportunities you can take advantage of on eBay, so we encourage everyone to give this program some attention. The performance-based nature of the program makes it affordable to experiment with as well.

To begin using eBay Keywords, you follow a three-step process:

1. **Register.**

2. **Create a campaign.**
   a. **Select a landing page.**
   b. **Create an ad.**
   c. **Select your keywords.**
   d. **Select your cost per click.**

3. **Monitor and manage your campaigns.**

To register for the program, go to this Web address and follow the instructions there:
http://www.ebaykeywords.com
Note that you must have at least one listing already in place to sign up for the program.

To show you how the program works, let's walk through a real-world setup of a campaign. In this example, we are going to create an eBay Keywords campaign for a Garmin eTrex GPS.

Once you have created your login, it's time to create a campaign. You will automatically be taken to the Create Campaign screen shown in Figure 6.7.

There are five choices to make to start the Create Campaign process:

1. **Name your campaign. Come up with a name for your campaign.**

2. **Enter a promo code. If you have a special promotion, enter the code here.**

3. **Set your campaign funds. How much you would like to budget to this campaign.**

4. **Establish your total funds. How much you have left in your account after the campaign allocation.**

5. **Choose an ad name. Name the ad you would like to have as part of the campaign.**

Once you have completed these steps, select "Create Ad," and you will be taken to the ad creation page shown in Figure 6.8.

As you see in Figure 6.8, the first choice is to select the landing page for the traffic that comes from your banner advertisement. The two choices are:

1. **Listing of all items. This sends traffic to the "View seller's items" page.**

2. **Particular item. This sends traffic to a specific listing.**

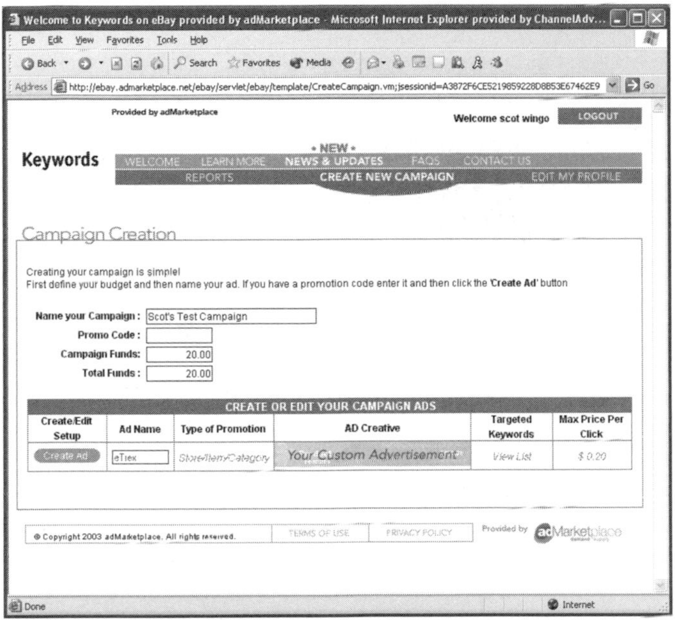

FIGURE 6.7 The Create Campaign screen

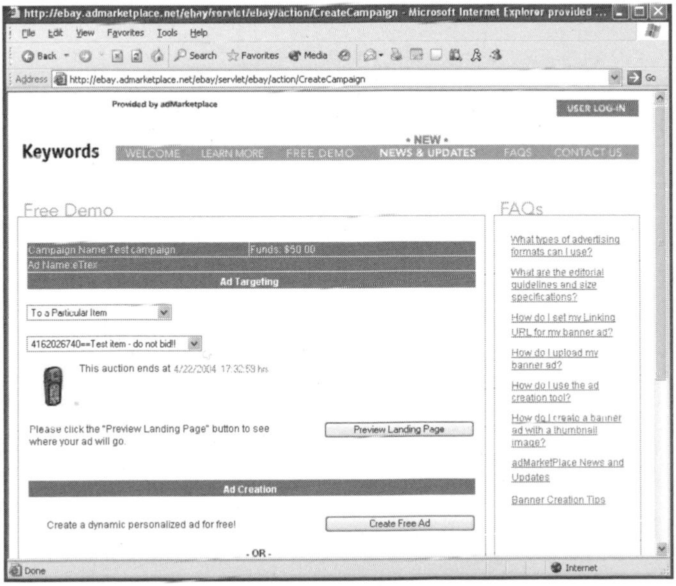

FIGURE 6.8 The eBay Keywords ad-creation page

There are pros and cons to each. With the "listing of items" approach, you can set up a campaign and keep it running for a long time without management. Conversely, with the "specific listing" option, your advertisements can be more specific but require management, because they will stop when the item expires.

For this example, we select the "particular item" option, as shown in Figure 6.8. Once you select this option, a list of your live listings is presented. When you select an item, as shown in Figure 6.8, the photo is automatically pulled from the listing, to be used for the rest of the advertisement creation process. After you have selected an item, the next step is ad creation, as illustrated in Figure 6.9.

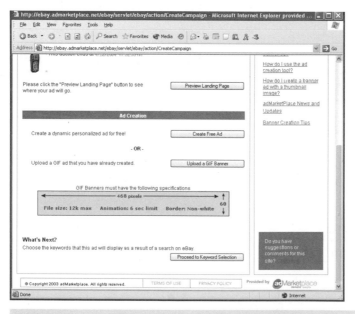

FIGURE 6.9   **The next steps of the eBay Keywords ad-creation process**

Next, you can choose to upload a precreated banner GIF file (468×60 pixels) or use the eBay Keywords banner creation tool. For this example, we will show you how to rapidly create an effective banner ad using the eBay Keywords banner creation tool. Selecting "Create Free Ad" takes you to the screen shown in Figure 6.10.

At this step in the process, you can choose from five different types of banners, all of which are self-explanatory. For advertising a single item, we have found the thumbnail banner to be very effective, so select that option. Now you are at step 2, as shown in Figure 6.11

As Figure 6.11 illustrates, some different options are available for the thumbnail-style banner ad. For this example, we pick the green one and then are taken to the third step, shown in Figure 6.12.

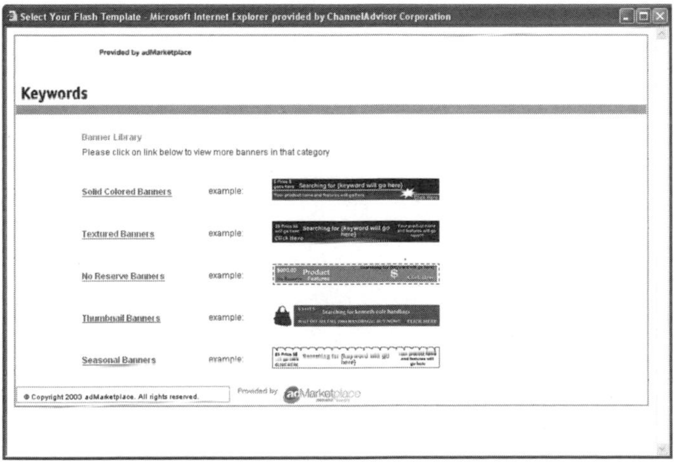

FIGURE 6.10   Step 1 of creating a free ad

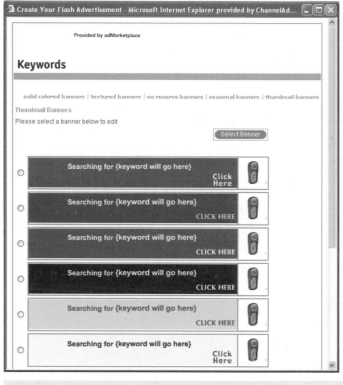

FIGURE 6.11 Create a free ad, step 2

In the third step, you customize the banner ad by entering both a short teaser that will be displayed in the upper left and a longer description that is displayed in the bottom of the ad. Note that the unchangeable text "Searching for *{search text goes here}*" will automatically be mapped to whatever the potential buyer searches on. For example, if the buyer searches on GPS, this will display "Searching for GPS" for that buyer.

Once the text has been entered, it can be previewed. Once you are satisfied with it, select "Create and upload banner." This takes you back to the Create Ad screen, but with the banner displayed, as shown in Figure 6.13.

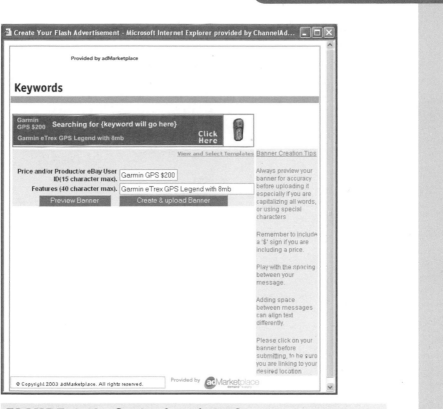

FIGURE 6.12   Create a free ad, step 3

Now that the ad-creation process is complete, select "Proceed to Keyword Selection," which takes you to the keyword screen, as shown in Figure 6.14.

On the keyword selection screen, you can manually enter your desired keywords (this is when it is useful to know the top keywords for your items, as mentioned earlier). Alternatively, you can upload a spreadsheet of keywords (in CSV format). The spreadsheet option is useful if you plan on running lots of campaigns and don't want to type in keywords repetitively.

For this example, we have entered some relevant terms and "dvd player" to illustrate an eBay Keywords trick (note

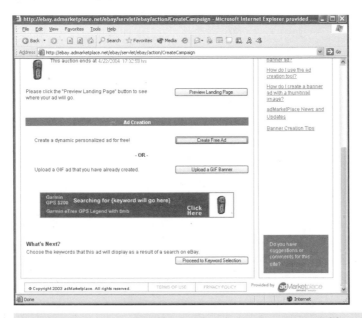

FIGURE 6.13   eBay Keywords ad-creation screen with custom banner displayed

FIGURE 6.14   The keyword selection screen for a campaign

that this keyword would not be allowed in reality, because it is not relevant to our product). As you will see, the trick is to use eBay Keywords to learn the popularity of various search terms and then leverage that information to optimize your titles—in addition to using the information in the eBay Keywords program.

When you select "Proceed to Price Selection," you are taken to the price comparison screen, shown in Figure 6.15.

The price comparison screen gives you a great deal of valuable information. First, you see the highest bid for each term entered. Notice in this example that "dvd player" is significantly higher than others. This is because there are more sellers competing for the term, which drives the price up as sellers bid for the top position by increasing their CPC.

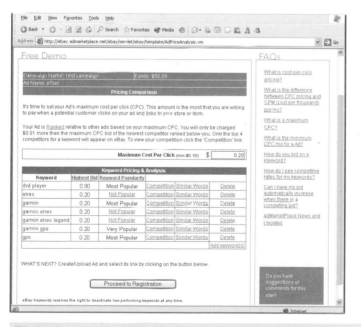

FIGURE 6.15   **The eBay Keywords price comparison screen**

The other valuable piece of information is "keyword popularity." This is extremely useful not only for your eBay Keywords campaign, but also for testing different keywords here, and using the results to decide which keywords should be in your auction titles.

The Competition link will allow you to see what other sellers are bidding for the same term. For example, if you click on the "dvd player" term, you will see the list shown in Figure 6.16.

On the keyword selection screen, you can enter the maximum CPC that you are willing to pay. Once you are done, you can submit your campaign for review and then for publication.

Testing Keyword Popularity

eBay Keywords takes the top 10,000 search terms on eBay and divides them into five groups:

1. Most popular—the top 2,500 terms

2. Very popular—the top 2,500 to 5,000 terms

3. Popular—the top 5,000 to 7,500 terms

4. Somewhat popular—the top 7,500 to 10,000 terms

5. Not popular—Not in the top 10,000 terms

The clever eBay promoter can use this tool to experiment with various keywords and determine the most popular. Then you can take that information and use it not only for the eBay Keywords program, but also to optimize your titles to include terms that are in the top 5,000 search terms on eBay.

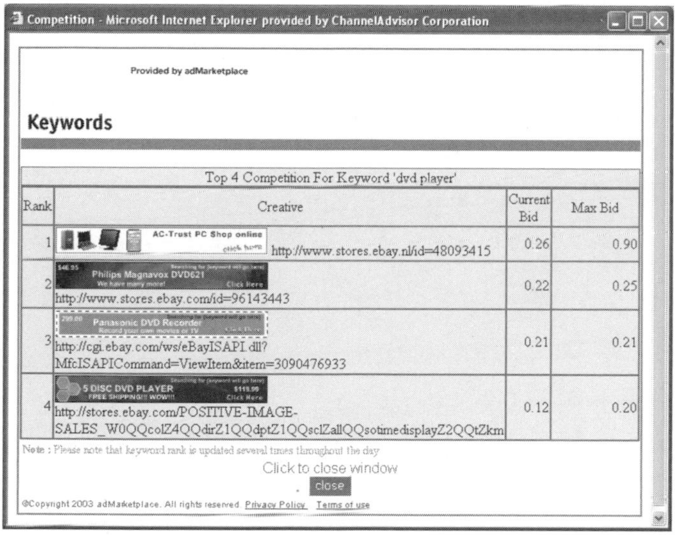

Rank	Creative	Current Bid	Max Bid
1	AC-Trust PC Shop online http://www.stores.ebay.nl/id=48093415	0.26	0.90
2	Philips Magnavox DVD621 http://www.stores.ebay.com/id=96143443	0.22	0.25
3	Panasonic DVD Recorder http://cgi.ebay.com/ws/eBayISAPI.dll?MfcISAPICommand=ViewItem&item=3090476933	0.21	0.21
4	5 DISC DVD PLAYER FREE SHIPPING!! WOW!!! http://stores.ebay.com/POSITIVE-IMAGE-SALES_W0QQcolZ4QQdirZ1QQdptZ1QQsclZallQQsotimedisplayZ2QQtZkm	0.12	0.20

FIGURE 6.16 Competitors for the term "dvd player"

Once you have had a campaign running for some time, the eBay Keywords program offers interesting real-time reporting of how your campaign is doing. Figure 6.17 shows an example of a live campaign report.

In Figure 6.17, there are several interesting results. First, the terms "dvd player" and "gps" do not have a high CPC and, therefore, are not being seen very often. Although the other terms are active, some are performing better than others. The number of impressions tells you how many times the banner has been viewed, and the click rate shows you what percentage of those banner views results in clicks to your item. Notice that the highest click rate is for the most specific term, which is frequently the case, because buyers click on more relevant advertisements.

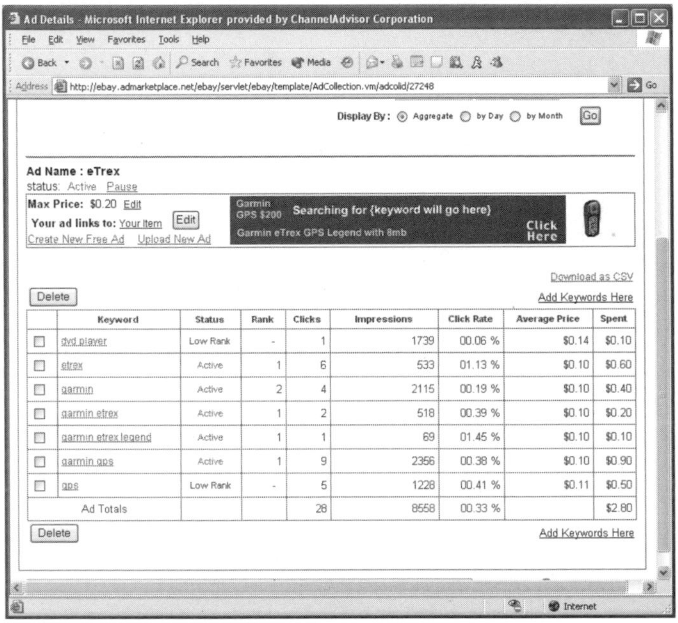

	Keyword	Status	Rank	Clicks	Impressions	Click Rate	Average Price	Spent
☐	dvd player	Low Rank	-	1	1739	00.06 %	$0.14	$0.10
☐	etrex	Active	1	6	533	01.13 %	$0.10	$0.60
☐	garmin	Active	2	4	2115	00.19 %	$0.10	$0.40
☐	garmin etrex	Active	1	2	518	00.39 %	$0.10	$0.20
☐	garmin etrex legend	Active	1	1	69	01.45 %	$0.10	$0.10
☐	garmin gps	Active	1	9	2356	00.38 %	$0.10	$0.90
☐	gps	Low Rank	-	5	1228	00.41 %	$0.11	$0.50
	Ad Totals			28	8558	00.33 %		$2.80

FIGURE 6.17 Sample report for a live eBay Keywords campaign

For this example, we have spent $2.80 and received 28 clicks to the item. Compared with the Highlight or Featured options, eBay Keywords gives you more performance-based information.

A Special Offer for Readers of This Book

We have secured a special eBay Keywords offer for readers of *eBay™ Strategies*. Details can be found at the *eBay™ Strategies* online blog and group:

Blog: http://ebaystrategies.blogs.com

Group: http://groups.ebay.com/forum.jspa?forumID=100006604

Browsing

As mentioned, while 80% of buyers use search to find items, a significant portion, 20%, actually browse through the eBay listings to find items. eBay has started a program in which it is drastically changing the way many categories are designed to favor item specifics (that is, attributes) rather than the traditional category structure. For example, at the time of this writing, eBay "rolled up" hundreds of CD and game categories into one mega-category that is too cumbersome to browse. The intent is to have buyers search by attributes instead.

For example, if previously buyers would browse the "Bluegrass" category, they now search using the genre attribute set to "bluegrass" and then browse through the results.

As this change propagates throughout all of eBay, the percentage of buyers who browse will go down, and the buyer experience will be almost pure search. Even given this change, it's important to make sure that your items show up when buyers browse, because the change will take a significant amount of time to roll out, and it may not affect all categories (such as collectibles).

How Browsers Browse

We have gathered significant amounts of data on buyer behavior, and we've found that the majority of browsers follow a simple practice:

1. **They start at ebay.com and select a category from the left side of the page.**

2. **They then keep "drilling down" until they reach a category of interest.**

3. Next, they either sort by a key factor for them, such as price, or simply start paging through auctions, looking for something interesting.

For example:

1. Start at ebay.com and select Toys and Hobbies.

2. Under Action Figures, select Star Wars, then Vintage, then "Star Wars: A New Hope," and then Vehicles.

3. Now sort by price.

More sophisticated browsers will bookmark the category page or use the "refine search" to eliminate words or narrow to a price range, and so on.

When thinking about promoting your items to browsers, the most important decision is the category in which you place your item. The key here is to be very specific. Many buyers, especially in collectibles, count on you to select the right category. For example, many buyers would not make it into "Action Figures/Star Wars/Vintage/Other" to look for an item.

Once the buyer gets to her desired category and starts browsing, listings are displayed by default according to their end time (soonest to latest). Thus, just as with search, timing with browsing is important.

Multiple Categories

eBay provides a feature that lets you list an item in two categories simultaneously. This feature is not free: the cost is a doubling of any listing fees and upgrades (but not final value fees). eBay says listing in multiple categories can increase the end price of your item by as much as 18%.

If this is the case, here is a formula for figuring out the ASP breakeven for considering the feature. Let's say you are using Gallery and you start your item at $9.99. Thus, your listing fee for multiple categories increases by $0.25 + $0.35 = $0.60.

$$18\% \times x = 0.60$$
$$x = \$3.33$$

Based on the 18% increase in price, if your item is $3.33 or greater, then it makes sense to consider multiple category listings.

In practice, however, we have found the results to be mixed. The best results come when an item can be multi-categorized into two very high traffic categories. For example, if you place a Garmin GPS device in the Consumer Electronics subcategory as well as a Sporting Goods or even Automotive category, then the extra traffic generated most likely will work.

However, listing a Star Wars action figure in both "Star Wars: A New Hope" and "Other" is not a good strategy.

As with search, some auction-management systems provide advanced functionality that lets you measure the traffic that originates from browsing, including the category browsed, so you can formulate more of an apples-to-apples picture of which categories do best, and if you should list in multiple categories.

Listing Upgrades

Once the buyer gets to her desired category, she will see listing results in the order that they would appear with the search engine. Therefore, the same listing upgrade behaviors and recommendations already covered apply here as well.

8 BUILD YOUR EBAY BRAND

Many eBay sellers believe their brand on eBay is basically their seller ID, their feedback points, and perhaps a logo. As more and more sellers take part in eBay, including large manufacturers and retailers, to stay competitive, sellers of all sizes have to build and present the best possible brand.

In fact, our research has shown that when presented with more than one seller with feedback above 1,000 and 99%, buyers decide based on brand rather than the highest feedback or the percentage above 99% of positive feedbacks. Creating, building, and maintaining a strong brand on eBay is one of the most important things you can do promotionally.

What is a great eBay brand? A brand is the sum of many things:

- **Your company name**

- **Your logo**

- **Your "look and feel"**

- **Your service levels**

- **Your feedback**

- **Your policies**

If you've spent much time shopping on eBay, you have probably seen some really bad brands. Dancing money on fire, text that follows cursors, poor color combinations, all-capital-letter descriptions, store names that make no sense, and so on.

In this section, we'll show some best practices for improving your eBay brand. MobilePC is used as an example, and they are also the case study for the chapter.

Listing Design

Potential buyers first encounter your brand in a listing. Therefore, the design, layout, and look and feel of every listing are very important.

Figure 6.18 shows a model auction design. The first thing you notice about this listing is the MobilePC brand. As the brand implies, MobilePC sells only portable computing devices, such as notebooks, laptops, and PDAs.

FIGURE 6.18   A sample listing by MobilePC

Next, you clearly see the links to About Us, Guarantee, Payment, Shipping, FAQS, and CheckOut Now!. Having these important components of the listing available at the top of the page and prominently displayed gives buyers all of the information they need, right at their fingertips.

Next, you will notice a clear and informative product image and an award that the seller has won from eBay. Also, notice the amount of detail provided on the item being sold, including the clear layout in table format of all the features of the product.

For comparison purposes, we ran a search for the same product shown in Figure 6.18. The listing we found is shown in Figure 6-19.

Compare the listing in Figure 6.19 to that in Figure 6.18. The first thing you notice is the poor layout of the second listing. There is no white space, and the seller's ID has not been provided. The product image is taken on a carpet, and it's not very appealing. Finally, the product features are presented in a jumbled list that is essentially unreadable.

If you were a buyer, which of these sellers would you do business with?

The About Me Page

About two years ago I got into a discussion with a seller about eBay's "About Me" pages. The seller believed that they were not useful and didn't even have one. I felt that they were another way sellers can promote their brand on eBay, but I didn't have much evidence of that. Eventually, we were able to record and monitor the traffic to auction

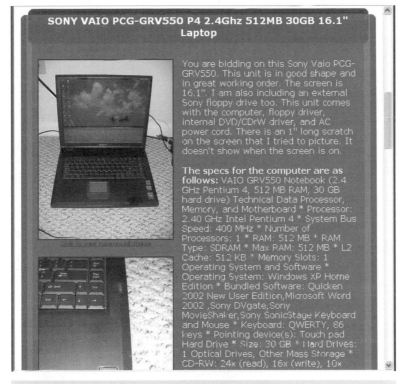

FIGURE 6.19   Another Sony Vaio GRV550

listings and About Me pages. Much to our surprise, About Me pages receive significant traffic. The way the traffic typically flows is the buyer finds a listing for the seller and goes to the About Me to learn more.

Based on this documented buyer behavior, the About Me page can be an effective way to build your brand and drive sales. Figure 6.20 shows MobilePC's About Me page.

Notice how similar the branding and layout here are to the auction listing. Also, there are some nice buyer features, such as the Search by Brand and Product Category on the left-hand side. In the center is a "Deal of the Week."

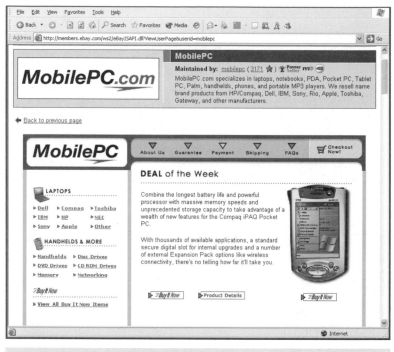

FIGURE 6.20   MobilePC's About Me page

A deal of the week/day/month is a great way to promote a featured SKU and drive GMS from the About Me page.

Once you've designed an effective About Me page, then you can link to it prominently in your listings. For example, the MobilePC "About Us" link goes to their About Me page. Or if you run any promotions outside of eBay, this is a great landing spot for external traffic, versus a more temporary listing. Also you have more control over the About Me than over other stores, such as eBay Stores.

eBay Stores

If you have an eBay Store, you should also extend your brand there, because, like the About Me page, buyers who find your listings will frequently navigate to your store and need to have your brand reinforced. Figure 6.21 shows the MobilePC eBay Store design.

In the eBay Store, you have the same MobilePC branding: the logo, the description, and finally the categories of products offered.

An appealing gallery style has been chosen by MobilePC for the eBay Store layout. At the time of this writing, eBay recently announced more options for eBay Stores, including more customizable pages.

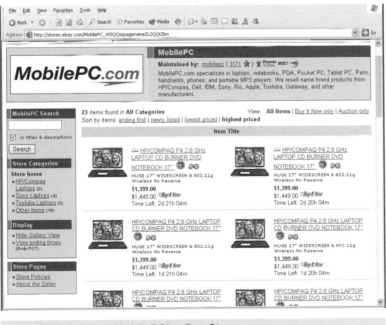

FIGURE 6.21   **MobilePC's eBay Store**

Opt-in E-mail Newsletter

Some sellers who really want to build their brand and promote their items enable buyers and potential buyers to subscribe to an opt-in e-mail newsletter. These newsletters can be informational or oriented purely toward product sales. Figure 6.22 shows an example of a seller who offers this feature.

Note that before you offer such a newsletter, you should familiarize yourself with spam laws and make sure you have processes in place for managing requests from people who want to unsubscribe and for managing other aspects of the newsletter. There are literally hundreds of services available to manage these types of newsletter lists.

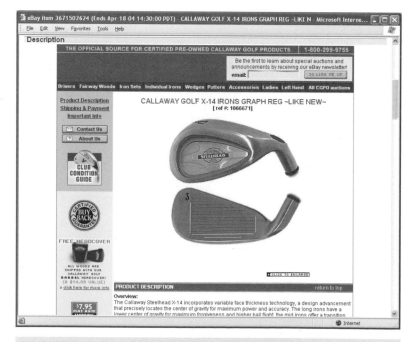

FIGURE 6.22 Seller with an e-mail newsletter sign-up in all auction listings

Don't Skimp on Design

eBay provides basic "listing designer" and "About Me page designer" tools to help you create a basic listing and About Me page. We recommend taking the additional time to create custom HTML that raises your brand to the next level.

Many companies will create the HTML for you. Graphic designers available on http://www.elance.com (an eBay professional services partner) can help you create a quality design for your eBay business.

Pulling It All Together

From the listing to the About Me page and the eBay Store, your brand should be consistent and clear. There are other opportunities for you to promote your brand, as well. If you don't use eBay's checkout, you can display your brand on your checkout. Also, you might want to consider having your brand printed on all of your shipping boxes, as well as on the invoice.

Case Study

MobilePC

Seller: mobilepc (3171 ⭐) 🏆Power Seller me 🔧

At COMDEX, CES, and other industry trade shows, eBay will frequently invite top sellers in a category to meet with management
and learn about eBay's plans for the future. At every one of these
events, dubbed "Seller Summits," eBay has an awards ceremony.
In late 2002, MobilePC won the award for best merchandiser.

If you'll review their listings, we think you'll find they have one of
the strongest, most consistent brands on eBay.

eBay Vitals

- **GMS**: $300,000–$400,000 per month
- **ASP**: $600–$800
- **CR**: 70–80%
- **Feedback**: 98.2%
- Top laptop/notebook seller

Background

In the late 1990s, Craig Zimmer worked for a company that
processed open-box returns. He led their group in charge of selling
items on eBay. In October of 2001, after the demise of the previous
company, he decided to start his own eBay business. He started
with the seller ID "pocketpcdeals," based on his early success in
selling PDAs using Microsoft's PocketPC operating system.

The business took off and expanded in product and thus outgrew
the "pocketpcdeals" name. He changed the name to "Laptops!"
The company still sold PDAs in addition to laptops, so ultimately
Craig decided to change the name one last time to "MobilePC" to
capture the company's focus on mobile technology in general,
from PDAs to laptops and notebooks. MobilePC now has more
than six employees and is based in California.

MobilePC and Promotion

Figures 6.18, 6.20, and 6.21 show some of MobilePC's branding. By focusing on their brand and maximizing eBay promotions, MobilePC regularly achieves ASPs and velocity 10 to 30% higher than other sellers in the same category with the same SKUs. We've already covered MobilePC's branding in detail.

The first and most important thing MobilePC does to promote its business is optimize every title for their auctions, making sure the titles use all of the available characters and include top eBay search terms. Figure 6.23 shows some examples of MobilePC's optimized titles.

You'll also notice that MobilePC utilizes subtitles, which makes sense given their high ASP and the fact they have some great things to say in subtitles, such as stating that they provide warranties. Additionally, for hot items of which they have deep quantities, MobilePC will frequently use Gallery, Featured Plus! and

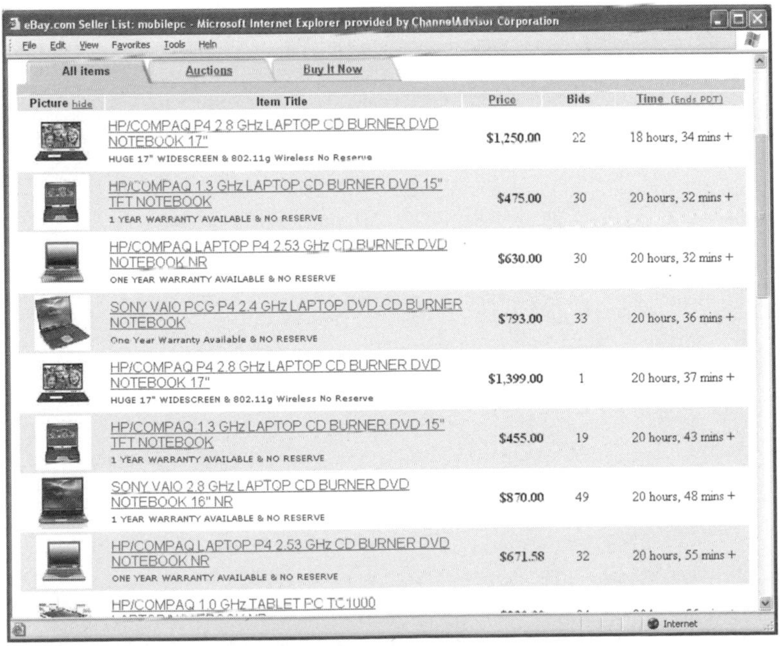

FIGURE 6.23 MobilePC's auction titles

Highlight upgrades. Figure 6.24 shows a search on eBay for a "Sony Vaio P4." Can you tell which listings are MobilePC's?

If you guessed listings 2, 3, and 4, you are correct! Any buyer searching on this term will have to work hard not to buy from MobilePC. MobilePC also offers gift services (and uses the gift icon) such as express shipping and gift wrapping.

Finally, MobilePC experiments with any available promotional program eBay offers. For example, they are a heavy participant in eBay Keywords. MobilePC also leverages the eBay Anything Points and warranty programs.

Other Strategies of Interest

On top of promotional excellence, MobilePC also pushes the envelope on pricing strategy. They are a heavy user of the Second Chance Offer and perception-of-scarcity strategies detailed in Chapter 5.

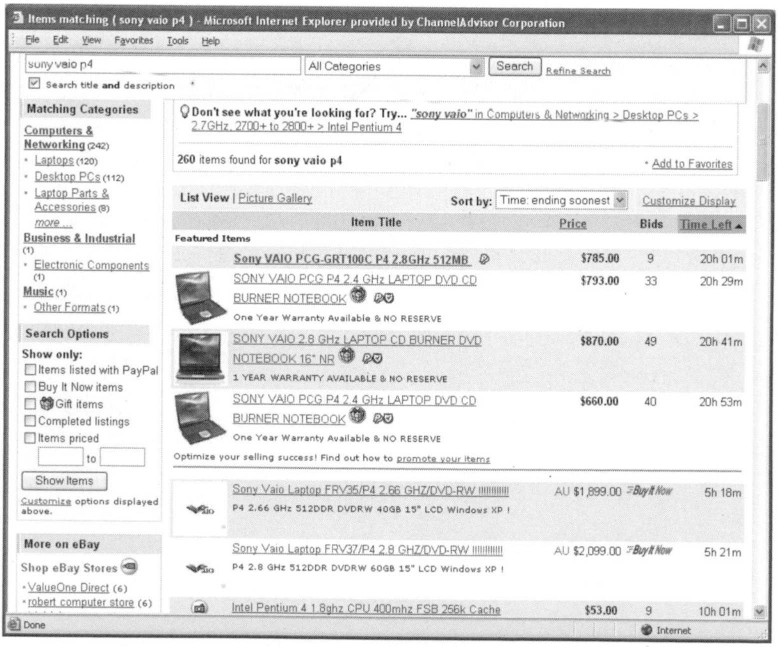

FIGURE 6.24   Guess which listings belong to MobilePC

Chapter 6 Summary

NEW TERMINOLOGY

Return on investment (ROI)—A term used by marketing professionals to refer to the value of promotions. For example, if you spend $200 on promotions that drive $2,000 in sales, you had an ROI of 10. In other words, you received ten times the value of the investment in return.

eBay Keywords—A new program eBay has introduced that allows sellers to strategically place banner ads in response to eBay buyer searches.

KEY CONCEPTS

In this chapter we covered all of the promotional opportunities available to an eBay business. By increasing the demand for your products, smart promotions extend the price/velocity curve, increasing your ASP and allowing you to sell more of the same unit without suffering price decreases.

The most important promotional tool at your disposal is the eBay search engine, which is used by 80% of buyers to find their items. By optimizing your listings to use all 55 characters available and to target the highest trafficked terms, you can dramatically increase the number of buyers who see your listings. Listing upgrades such as Subtitle, Gift Services, Featured Plus!, and Bold are also available, but they should be used wisely to make sure there is a positive ROI.

eBay Keywords gives sellers a performance-based system that should be seriously considered.

In addition to the search engine optimization, sellers should carefully consider the categories where they place their items, because the other 20% of buyers find items by browsing. Listing upgrades also show up when buyers are browsing categories.

Finally, building a consistent and clear eBay brand for every part of your eBay business helps promote not only

Chapter 6 Summary

your items but also your entire company. In addition to clear branding on your listings, you should consider extending the branding to your About Me page, eBay Store, and any other places where you "touch" the customer. For example, you should consider investing in branded boxes and a branded e-mail newsletter.

EXERCISES

1. Spend two hours researching top search terms in your category and then make sure you have them in your titles.

2. Try listing in new but valid categories. Do you see any differences in the ASP for these items?

3. Test out the eBay Keywords program. Do you get a positive ROI?

4. Do a search for a product on eBay. Look at five different sellers' branding and give them a grade. How does your brand compare?

5. Buy something from Amazon.com. How many times do you experience their brand? What does their brand "stand for"? What can you learn from their brand "best practices" that you can apply to your own business?

eBay

SEVEN

Placement

The fourth P in the strategic eBay framework: placement

T he fourth *P* in the Five P's is *placement*. Placement refers to the decision you make whenever you sell a product: where to place, or offer, your item. If you recall, in Chapter 6, we touched on categories and scheduling. Those are the key placement decisions when you decide to sell an item on eBay. However, in Chapter 4, we introduced the concept of the product life cycle and the eBay sweet spot. The product life cycle shows that eBay may not be the best place for all of your products. In fact, since eBay buyers come to eBay for a significant discount from retail, you will most likely find it a challenge to make margin on in-season items you may source.

Also, not all Internet buyers are on eBay. Although eBay has an impressive 90 million registered users and 45 million active users, other venues such as Yahoo! and Amazon.com have similar active user numbers. Several services track the users of eBay, Yahoo!, and Amazon.com, and they show that the overlap in these companies' audiences is relatively small: in the range of 20 to 40%.

Both of these points add up one fact: If you have an "eBay only" strategy, you are not only missing out on a large part of the online audience and potential buyers, but also restricting the type of product you are able to sell to end-of-life and liquidation product.

This chapter explores the strategic importance of placement, not only on eBay, but also on other marketplaces that let you increase sales while reaching a new audience— and potentially selling different types of products than those that sell well only on eBay.

eBay Placement

W hen selling on eBay, you have several placement decisions to make: the category, the time, the duration, and the seller name under which you list your products.

Category

In Chapter 6, we touched on the importance of selecting the categories most highly trafficked by browsers. One way to research the best category is to use eBay's completed item search for similar SKUs. Once you have found the historic listings that most closely match what you have to sell, check the category selection on the historic listings with the highest ASPs achieved.

Alternatively, you may want to consider using software that lets you measure the traffic to your items (from both browsers and searchers). Then you can compare the results by testing items in various categories to see which get the best results.

As mentioned in Chapter 6, you can also list your item in multiple categories concurrently. In our experience, this rarely pays for the extra listing fee. The exception to that rule is items that can span two completely different categories.

For example:

- **Multi-listing in the Consumer Electronics > Gadgets and Consumer Electronics > PDAs category will not have a positive ROI 99% of the time.**

- **With a pair of Nike golf shoes, it probably makes sense to list in both of these categories:**
  - **Sporting Goods and Fan Shop > Golf > Shoes, Sandals > Men > Nike**
  - **Clothing, Shoes & Accessories > Men's Shoes**

Scheduling

On eBay, you need to plan timing wisely, because timing can positively (if done well) or negatively (if done poorly) influence your results by as much as 20 to 40% depending on the ASP. In Chapter 6, we discussed peak eBay traffic times:

1. **Weekend evenings.**

2. **Weekday evenings—in this order: Thursday, Friday, Wednesday, Tuesday, Monday.**

3. **During holidays, the lunch hours of 12:00 to 4:00 Eastern time have enough traffic to justify targeting them if you are relatively deep in inventory.**

You can use simple free counters as well as completed items to research the best timing for a SKU. Additionally, more advanced software may be available, to provide traffic source as well as the time the traffic came to the listing. Also, eBay now provides a scheduling service for $0.10 per listing, or you may find one of the advanced auction-management systems that offer this feature.

In addition to timing a listing to close at peak traffic times, another important scheduling decision is the duration or length of a listing. At the time of this writing, eBay offers listings of one, three, five, seven, and ten days. Note that ten-day listings incur an extra listing fee of $0.20.

One of the strategies you should constantly experiment with is duration. Many sellers experiment with various durations and come up with rules that work for them based on a SKU's CR, depth, ASP, and other factors.

Here are the general rules of thumb we have developed for duration:

■ **Ten-day listings.** When you have a very unusual auction that would benefit from prolonged exposure, the ten-day listing is the best option, and it's worth the extra $0.20. The benefit is you have three extra days for potential bidders on the unique item to discover it and join in the bidding or BIN.

- **Seven-day listings.** This is the average duration. Many sellers go seven days because they like to post on weekends and close on weekends. For a $1NR auction, this is the optimal time frame, because as we've seen, weekends tend to be peak traffic times, and traffic dramatically affects the results of a $1NR auction.

- **Five-day listings.** If your CR is above 50%, you can experiment with bringing the duration down to five or three days, to accelerate your velocity. Generally, a CR greater than 50% indicates there is adequate demand for your items to crank up the listing velocity somewhat.

- **Three-day listings.** If your CR is above 75%, it indicates there is adequate demand to explore a three-day-listing strategy. You can take all of your listings down to three days or do so on a per-SKU basis, depending on the SKU's CR.

- **One-day listings.** If you enjoy a CR above 85% or are very deep in an item and want to really accelerate the velocity, then one-day auctions are for you. Also, if you have "perishable" inventory, one-day listings can be helpful. For example, if you have event tickets, one-day auctions give you the opportunity to run auctions closer to the event than the other auction durations.

    One-day auctions are also a great promotional item. For example, Figure 7.1 illustrates a seller who uses one-day auctions to ask buyers, "Why wait to win?"

Seller Name/Seller ID

Another placement decision you may face when selling on eBay is what seller ID to sell under. This is a somewhat controversial topic. For example, some sellers feel strongly

FIGURE 7.1 **A one-day auction promotion by Sharper Image**

that you should have separate seller IDs—usually for various product categories. Other sellers are convinced that one seller ID helps accumulate feedback for the ID, versus a multi-seller ID strategy, which divides feedback among different IDs.

Who is right? Well, it depends on your business and your goals. Here are some reasons why you may want to try a multi-seller ID strategy:

■ **If you have different types of product, you may have different policies for each type of product. For example, you may have "new in box" product that carries a warranty. If you also carry refurbished product or "as-is" product with different terms and conditions, you should put those items under a different seller ID.**

- If you sell deeply in more than one category, you may want to build category-specific seller IDs so you can promote them differently. For example, if you sell CDs and video games, you may want to have seller IDs such as "MYCD-STORE" and "MYDVDSTORE." Perhaps your CD store's branding would be focused on music and you would promote it using eBay Keywords for top CD search terms. The DVD store would have a different look and feel and a different promotional strategy. You could optionally tie the stores together if you wanted to share traffic between the two and cross-promote.

- If you sell in different countries, you should probably separate the sales into country-specific seller IDs. This helps keep the buyers separate and avoids confusion about what products are available where. Also, it will help you with various taxation and international shipping issues you are likely to encounter.

- If you are not able to run reports by SKU type, by supplier, or by another important variable, you may want to use separate seller IDs to keep the buckets of inventory separate. Then you'll be able to use the seller IDs as the basis for reporting.

Even if you do have more than one seller ID, you can link them together using space on your auction listings and cross-promote.

9 EXPLORE OTHER CHANNELS

As mentioned in Chapter 4, the product life cycle largely determines what will sell well on eBay and what won't. The fact that only liquidation and end-of-life product sell well on eBay is due to the eBay buyer's behavior. It's a well-documented fact that (outside of collectibles and rare items) eBay buyers are typically looking for products at 20 to 50% off retail pricing.

But what if you have access to or have previously purchased product that you want to sell close to or at retail price? Fortunately, there are other marketplaces where buyers are less price sensitive, more interested in the latest and greatest, and willing to pay closer to retail.

Figure 7.2 shows the product life cycle with other Internet channels and where they fit into the mix.

The first thing you will notice is the addition of many new venues where you can sell your products. None of

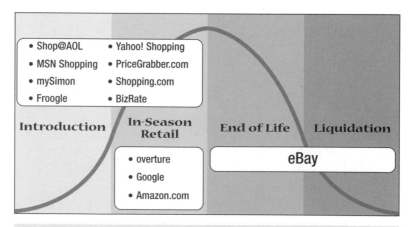

FIGURE 7.2   Product life cycle with other channels

these venues is an auction site like eBay. However, like eBay, they are "marketplaces" or, in other words, places where buyers and sellers come to meet. The only difference is that the price format is fixed rather than variable.

Many sellers have tried different auction sites without success. Thus, they come to believe that other market-places are a waste of time. Fortunately, over the years the fixed-price marketplaces have grown relatively big and are usually well worth the time. Although none of them may be as large as eBay for your business, if you can add two marketplaces that are as big as your eBay business in total, then you have essentially doubled your sales.

In addition to increasing sales, there are numerous other strategic benefits from selling via additional channels (called a multi-channel strategy):

- **Less competition. You will find as you try non-eBay channels that the competition typically isn't as fierce, resulting in higher ASPs. Part of this is the benefit of not having the auction format, which is a double-edged sword.**

- **Life cycle expansion. By adding new channels, you will be able to sell not only end-of-life and liquidation product, but also more in-season retail.**

- **Audience. Additional channels expose your products to a new audience of buyers whom you may not be reaching today.**

- **Fewer eBay-like challenges. Although eBay is a great channel, it can be very challenging. Issues such as NPBs, negative feedback, PayPal chargebacks, and so on can make you pull your hair out. You will find that other, fixed-price channels don't have these time-consuming issues. But there's no such thing as a free lunch either; you will have to work hard to be successful on *any* channel.**

Some negatives do come with a multi-channel strategy, however:

- **Focus.** By adding channels, if you do not have the bandwidth, you may lose focus on your eBay business.

- **Inventory management.** Managing multiple channels can be complex. One of the most complicated aspects is managing inventory across the various channels. If not done properly, you can end up either overselling or underselling your inventory.

- **Multiple order sources.** With multiple channels, you will also have multiple sources of orders. These orders will likely be very different from those you process on eBay, requiring new processes and procedures for handling the orders from the various new channels.

- **Different models from eBay.** Every online channel has its own intricacies and dynamics that will take you a while to learn. Based on the experience of top eBay sellers who have expanded into new channels, you should expect the learning curve for new channels to be about 50% of the eBay learning curve.

When to Go Multi-Channel

Given the complexities of going multi-channel, we recommend looking to expand to new channels only when you feel you have reached the maximum sales you can generate via eBay. There are several indicators that you have hit an eBay ceiling:

- **GMS fails to increase over the course of two quarters after you have used the Five P's framework to optimize your product, pricing, promotions, placement, and performance.**

- **GMS increases, but margin deteriorates three or more months in a row.**

- **ASPs drop rapidly, causing you to post substantially more items than before, which erodes margin.**

Every online channel that has proven to be effective could have their own books written about how to optimize them. Given space constraints, we briefly introduce the top channels and their basic concepts, then we point to more information for those interested in testing new channels. Note that although new channels are different from eBay, we have found that the Five P framework extends to these marketplaces. So, as you try new channels, think about:

- **The product you will sell**

- **How you will price the product**

- **Promoting the product**

- **On which marketplace you will place the product**

- **The performance**

Yahoo! Stores

One of the top portals on the Internet, Yahoo! is where more than 25% of Internet users call home. Most of these users use Yahoo! as their starting point to find products.

Yahoo! has a number of offerings that allow merchants to gain access to those buyers. One of the most popular offerings for eBay sellers is known as Yahoo! Stores.

Yahoo! recently renamed Yahoo! Stores to Yahoo! Small Business Merchant Solutions (YSBMS for short). YSBMS provides two pieces of functionality. The first is a hosted e-commerce site that sellers can manage through some useful tools. There are three levels of service offered by YSBMS, as shown in Table 7.1.

TABLE 7.1   Yahoo! SBMS service levels

PLAN	STARTER	STANDARD	PROFESSIONAL
Monthly fee	$39.95	$99.95	$299.95
Setup fee	$50.00	$50.00	$50.00
Transaction fee	1.5%	1.0%	0.75%

We recommend that sellers start with the Starter plan and move up when the economics work in your favor. In the higher-cost plans, the decreasing transaction fee covers the increased monthly fee at larger GMS values. On its own, YSBMS provides a robust e-commerce store. But simply setting up a YSBMS store does not bring buyers to your store.

To generate buyer interest, the second piece of functionality available to YSBMS stores pushes your inventory so it is seen in the Yahoo! Shopping area. YSBMS store owners get a 20% discount when advertising on Yahoo! Shopping from a YSBMS store.

Your YSBMS store automatically can push inventory to Yahoo! Shopping on your behalf. The traffic is then routed to your YSBMS store.

As with the different plans, there is a point where your transaction costs will become high enough that you may want to consider moving your e-commerce to a less-expensive platform and paying the extra 20% to advertise in Yahoo! Shopping.

For more details on all that YSBMS has to offer, see:

http://smallbusiness.yahoo.com/merchant/

Amazon.com

Over the years, Amazon.com has offered numerous ways to allow small businesses to gain access to their more than 40 million active buyers. First, there was Amazon Auctions, then there was zShops, and most recently, they have introduced the Amazon Marketplace.

We recommend that even if you have tried Amazon Auctions or zShops in the past without success, try Amazon Marketplace now.

Amazon Marketplace allows you first to identify a SKU on Amazon.com and then offer your inventory for sale. Then any Amazon shopper can find your item when he or she navigates to the SKU on Amazon.com. Amazon Marketplace solves many of the problems that kept Amazon Auctions from being successful. Amazon.com has discovered that their buyers first navigate to a SKU and then look at sellers, which is how Marketplace works. The zShops and Auction offerings only put results toward the bottom of the Amazon search results, producing very little, if any, traffic.

Figure 7.3 shows a popular SKU in the Amazon.com consumer electronics category.

Notice in Figure 7.3 the link that says "17 used & new from $54.88." When you click on that link, you are taken to

©2002 Amazon.com, Inc. All Rights Reserved.

FIGURE 7.3   SanDisk 256MB card on Amazon.com

all the sellers for the item. There are two classes of sellers. First, Featured Merchants are displayed. Amazon reserves the Featured Merchant designation for their large partners that use offerings they call Merchants.com and Merchants@.

Below the Featured Merchants, Amazon Marketplace results are displayed. Figure 7.4 shows the Featured Merchants for the SanDisk 256MB card.

Notice that, like eBay, each Marketplace merchant has a feedback rating and is able to describe the product they are selling and name a price, condition, and shipping options. Once you have evaluated Amazon.com, the next frontier is your own e-commerce site.

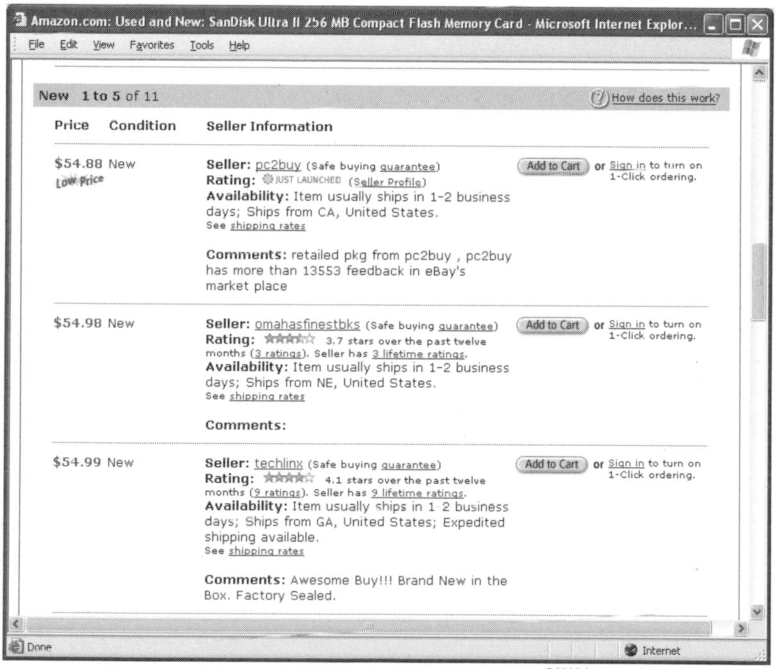

FIGURE 7.4   Amazon Marketplace sellers for SanDisk 256MB card

Your Own E-Commerce Site

Most sellers start expanding beyond eBay by opening their own e-commerce site. There are thousands of options for creating your own e-commerce site, including going with a site provided by your auction-management software company, arranging an account through your ISP, or developing your own custom site.

Unfortunately, most sellers become frustrated when their new site gets very little traction and generates little or no sales. The missing key to success is traffic (buyers). All great e-commerce sites promote themselves heavily through a variety of avenues, which we'll now introduce.

The following sections detail the top ways to promote your own e-commerce site.

SEARCH ENGINES

Most Internet buyers begin their online search for a product by going to either Yahoo!, Google, MSN, or AOL. Within these search engines, there are two types of results:

1. **Algorithmic. Also called organic or natural. These results are generated by an index maintained by the search engine. A proprietary algorithm determines the results shown. There are companies, called search engine optimization firms (SEOs), that try to figure out how the algorithms work and change your site to show up higher on the list. Results with this approach are very mixed and usually not worth the investment.**

2. **Paid search. Also called paid search or pay per click (PPC). Usually on the top of the page, on the side, or both, today's search engines generate revenue by providing "sponsored listings" in addition to the algorithmic listings. With these listings, advertisers pay on a per-click basis via an auction process that determines their ranking on the site.**

One popular analogy states that algorithmic search is like the white pages and paid search is like the yellow pages. The primary difference is that when you advertise in the yellow pages, you don't know if you'll get any phone calls. With paid search, you pay only when someone clicks on the link, generating traffic to your site (which you still have to convert, but it's one step closer to the transaction than a "view"). If yellow pages were like paid search in the off-line world, you would pay only when someone walked in your store or called you after reading your yellow page advertisement!

There are three major players in the paid-search space:

- **Google.** Google's paid-search program is called AdWords. Google powers AOL, Ask Jeeves, EarthLink, Amazon's A9, and several other popular search engines' paid listings.

- **Overture.** Overture, which was recently acquired by Yahoo!, pioneered the concept of paid search. In addition to Yahoo!, Overture powers MSN, Search.com, AltaVista, FAST, and many more.

- **FindWhat.** The smallest of the three, but also very economical, FindWhat.com powers many second-tier search engines, such as Terra Lycos and many others.

At the time of this writing, it is widely known that Microsoft's MSN division will be coming out with its own paid-search offering before the end of 2004. When that service is released, it will compete with Google's and Overture's paid-search offerings.

Figure 7.5 shows a Yahoo! search results page. The non-navigation portion of the page starts with "Inside Yahoo!". This section drives searchers into the Yahoo! Shopping shopping engine. The "Sponsor Results" shows four paid listings. Yahoo! lists the advertiser's name along with a description of what they have to offer. On the right-hand side (in boxes) are more paid results. At the bottom of the page, you see the start of a section called "Top 20 Web Results"—those are the algorithmic results.

Reviewing this page, you quickly see why more and more traffic is going to paid listings or through shopping engines and not into algorithmic results. The top areas are

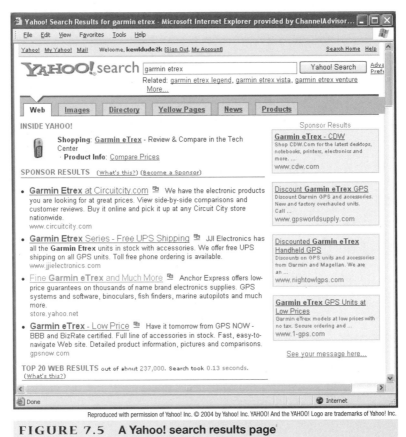

Reproduced with permission of Yahoo! Inc. © 2004 by Yahoo! Inc. YAHOO! And the YAHOO! Logo are trademarks of Yahoo! Inc.

FIGURE 7.5   A Yahoo! search results page

all sponsored listings (paid) compared to the algorithmic Web search results lower on the page.

Figure 7.6 shows a Google search results page. At the top of the page in the colored bands are two Sponsored Links. On the right, you see boxes with more Sponsored Links. Underneath the top colored links, the first section contains links to Google's shopping engine, Froogle. Beneath the Froogle links, Google's algorithmic results begin.

If you would like to learn more about paid search, all the paid-search sites provide introductory offers as well as detailed instructions and tutorials on how their programs work.

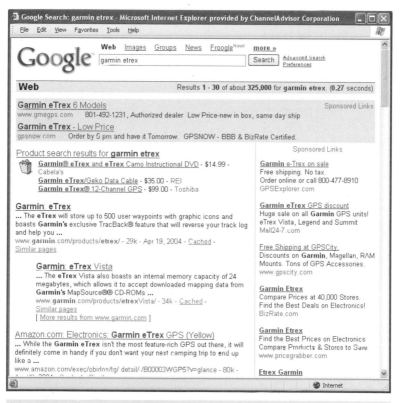

FIGURE 7.6 A Google search results page

SHOPPING ENGINES

As you can see from the results in Figures 7.5 and 7.6, the portals and search engines tend to drive traffic to shopping engines as well as to paid-search listings. In addition to the portal shopping engines (such as MSN Shopping, Shop@AOL, Yahoo! Shopping, Froogle), there are several independent shopping engines that are very popular, including mySimon, Shopping.com, PriceGrabber.com, NexTag, and BizRate.

Shopping engines give buyers an interface to find a SKU and then compare the price and other aspects of various merchants that offer that SKU. Figure 7.7 shows a typical shopping engine results page.

At the top of Figure 7.7, you see product information about the SKU being searched for. The box to the right shows that 40 merchants offer the product and there's a price range of $158.00 to $249.99. Underneath "Compare prices," you see that the merchants are listed. Most shopping engines sort the merchant results based on a pay-per-

FIGURE 7.7 A Shopping.com results page for the **Garmin eTrex GPS SKU**

click first; the consumer must choose to sort the items by price, if desired. In Figure 7.7, for example, CompWest USA appears to be paying the most per click and thus shows up at the top of the rankings.

Unlike paid search, in shopping engines, merchants bid on a category basis and not by keyword or SKU. Some merchants have generated a very strong ROI by bidding to the top three slots. Others focus on having the lowest price, believing that most buyers immediately sort the results list by price.

AFFILIATE PROGRAMS

You are probably aware of Amazon.com's Associate program. In what's generically called an affiliate program, Web site owners can direct buyers of books or any other Amazon product to the Amazon site, in exchange for a revenue share (from 5 to 15%) of completed orders. There are companies that will help you set up your own affiliate program, so that you too, like Amazon.com, can enlist Web site owners to promote your store, in exchange for a revenue share.

The two main companies are LinkShare and Commission Junction (also known as CJ). Some Internet marketing managers swear by affiliate programs, while others have found they are not worth the complexity of managing them and feel their efforts are better spent elsewhere.

E-MAIL NEWSLETTERS

Regardless of the channel on which you sell, you are ultimately acquiring customers. One of the highest-ROI actions you can take for your own e-commerce site is to e-mail frequent deals or offers to your most valuable asset: your customer base. Literally hundreds of companies provide great customer management/e-mail management software that allows you to track who reads your newsletters, manage opt-ins and opt-outs, and measure performance metrics such as opens, clicks, and conversions. Popular providers for smaller businesses are Topica and Roving.

Caution: Handle E-mail with Care

Given the backlash on spam that has resulted in legislation calling for large penalties for spammers, if you plan on offering an e-mail newsletter it's important to do the following:

- Make it very clear to your customers they are opting in to your newsletter.

- Provide and manage unsubscribe functionality.

- State clear policies on how you plan to handle customers' e-mail information.

Putting It All Together

After eBay, the least expensive way to test some of the techniques introduced in this chapter is to go with a Yahoo! Store or a similarly inexpensive offering and start experimenting. First, we would recommend shopping engines, because they are relatively low maintenance and easy to measure. Next, you should learn about paid search. Finally, you can expand into Amazon.com and affiliate programs, potentially moving from a simple store to a more complex offering.

CrazyApe

Seller: crazyape (26668 ⭐) 🏆Power Seller m🖫 ⦿

I first heard of CrazyApe when a package came to our office. The receptionist announced, "Bill, you have a package from CrazyApe." Everyone in the office cracked up because of the zany name. Bill had ordered some educational software for his kids on the Internet from a company named CrazyApe. Being a frequent purchaser of software, I checked out the company and, much to my surprise, found them everywhere. I ordered several titles.

Weeks later, one of the founders called, and we got to know their business very well. What we quickly learned is the folks at CrazyApe are not crazy; there is a method to their madness, and part of that method is very smart placement.

eBay Vitals

- **GMS**: $10,000–$20,000 per month (on eBay); 10–20 times that on other channels
- **ASP**: $10–$20
- **CR**: 35–40%
- **Feedback**: 99.3%
- Sells more than 1,000 items per month on eBay alone

Background

Based in Minnesota, CrazyApe started selling computer hardware equipment on eBay in 1998. In 1999 and 2000, they shifted their model from computer hardware to software, because they found there was less competition.

As their sales on eBay grew, CrazyApe wanted to grow even faster and started exploring other channels. This strategy significantly increased their business. They discovered that some of the other channels performed as well as or better than eBay.

Unfortunately, about a year ago, CrazyApe faced a challenge on eBay: many of their listings were taken down because someone at eBay believed their software was not authentic. Fortunately, thanks to a multi-channel strategy, CrazyApe was able to keep selling on other channels while they fixed the problem.

Today, CrazyApe employs 10 to 15 people and is growing substantially every quarter.

Figure 7.8 shows CrazyApe's About Me page, and Figure 7.9 shows one of their popular items for sale.

FIGURE 7.8   CrazyApe's About Me page

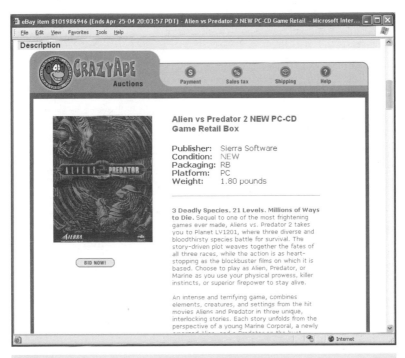

FIGURE 7.9   One of CrazyApe's items for sale

CrazyApe and Placement

The first step CrazyApe took when looking to expand into other channels was creating their own e-commerce site. CrazyApe chose to develop a custom e-commerce site, illustrated in Figure 7.10.

CrazyApe has tested numerous ways to drive traffic to their e-commerce site. Many of their "tricks" are proprietary, but here are the ones they would let us share.

AFFILIATE PROGRAM

CrazyApe implemented a very successful affiliate program. As you can see in Figure 7.11, like the rest of their branding, they make the affiliate program fun.

FIGURE 7.10 CrazyApe's e-commerce site

The result of the CrazyApe affiliate program is that buyers across the Internet come across their products. For example, in Figure 7.12, pretend you are reading about a new game on GameSpot.com, a popular gaming site. Right there on the game's page, you find a link to CrazyApe, where the game is conveniently for sale.

**Own A Website?
Wanna Make
Money?**

Affiliate Information
Click here

FIGURE 7.11
How CrazyApe
promotes their
affiliate program

SHOPPING ENGINES

In addition to the affiliate program, CrazyApe placed itself on the most popular shopping engines on the Internet, such as mySimon.

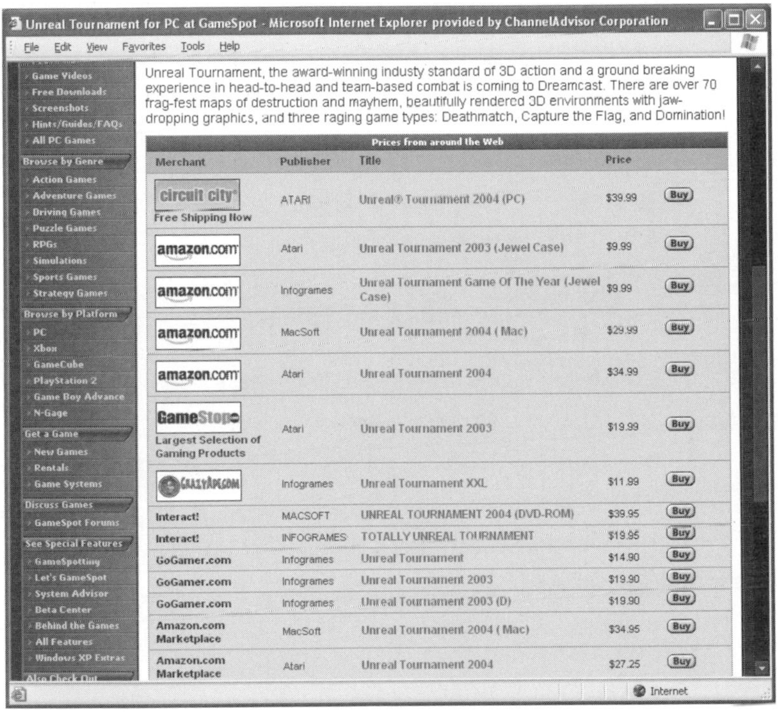

FIGURE 7.12   CrazyApe shown on GameSpot.com

NEWSLETTER

After trying new channels for several months, CrazyApe realized that they invest a considerable amount of money acquiring new customers and thus needed to maximize that investment. They started an opt-in newsletter program that has resulted in a very large increase in the revenue per customer and the ROI from the investment in customer acquisitions.

Other Strategies of Interest

CrazyApe realized early on that with discount software, the key is volume. To be able to support the volume growth they saw in their business, CrazyApe invested in a 40,000-square-foot, state-of-the-art logistics facility. This investment has paid off with very high customer ratings (for example, more than 99% positive on eBay). Also, as CrazyApe has explored new channels that have accelerated their business, they have never had to slow down to move to a new facility or deal with shipping or logistics problems.

From a promotion standpoint, although you may find the CrazyApe brand to be unusual, its uniqueness and fun nature make it very easy to remember and recognize. CrazyApe plays off their brand by putting the "crazy ape" on all of their branded materials, both online and off-line.

Finally, CrazyApe has great customer service, placing their toll-free number on literally every eBay listing, every page of their Web site, and all their materials, to encourage their customers to contact them.

Chapter 7 Summary

NEW TERMINOLOGY

Multi-channel—Term used to describe your business when you go from one channel (eBay is typically first) to many online channels (or at least more than one).

Search engine optimization (SEO)—Typically, service provided by a company that will "tweak" your Web site so that it shows up higher in the algorithmic portion of search engine results.

Pay per click (PPC)—A term used to describe paid-search programs in which you pay only when a potential buyer clicks on your listing or advertisement.

Affiliate program—A promotional program in which you offer revenue shares to other Web sites so that they will promote your products across the Internet.

KEY CONCEPTS

In this chapter, we covered the fourth *P* of the Five P's strategic framework: placement. There are two angles on placement: Choosing which marketplaces or channels on which to place your products and, if on eBay, where, how, and when to place listings within the eBay marketplace.

On the eBay side, the important strategic placement decisions are the category you choose, the scheduling you set up, and the seller ID you use. For category placement, you can test several categories to determine the best option for each of your SKUs. When testing, you may find two categories that are in different meta-categories (for example, not both under Computers, but maybe one in eBay Motors and one in Consumer Electronics). The decision on listing in multiple categories boils down to the ROI on the double listing fees that you pay, which will also be driven by your ASP.

Chapter 7 Summary

Optimized scheduling placement on eBay can dramatically increase your results, as most sellers have already discovered. In this chapter, we introduced general rules of thumb about how long to let auctions run and when to end them. However, every product and seller can have different results, so we encourage you to start with the rules of thumb and then optimize for your business and your products, on a SKU-by-SKU basis. This will be a highly effective use of your time and can result in a 10 to 15% increase in ASP when done methodically.

Finally, for eBay, many sellers have decided on a "multi-seller ID" strategy, in which they have several eBay seller brands or identities and distribute their products among them. Some distribute based on the category of the product, others on the condition of the product, and still others based on volume. The choice to be a single-seller ID business or a multi-seller ID business is largely based on your goals and product types.

If your sales on eBay have hit a plateau and you have worked through the Five P's strategy framework, the time has come to consider other online channels for your products. Though the learning curve will be steep, and it will require extra work and add complexities to your business, the results can help you dramatically grow your business while reducing competition and business risk.

Here are the top alternative channels to consider.

Yahoo! Stores

Now formally called Yahoo! Small Business Merchant Solutions (YSBMS, for short), this is a quick and relatively inexpensive way to create your own e-commerce site that is hosted and powered by Yahoo! One of the benefits of setting up a YSBMS store is the ability to get traffic from the shop-

Chapter 7 Summary

ping and Web search areas of the Yahoo! portal and gain experience with those concepts within a "starter" environment.

The YSBMS economics typically work out such that it will pay to go to your own e-commerce site eventually. If you don't want to go through the switch, then instead of starting with YSBMS, you may want to consider going straight to your own e-commerce solution.

Amazon.com

Amazon.com has numerous offerings for sellers. We recommend trying the Amazon Marketplace. To start, simply find a SKU you want to sell on Amazon Marketplace and click the "Sell Yours Here" link to place your item for sale.

Your Own E-Commerce Site

One of the top "off eBay" channels you should explore is having your own e-commerce site. Before you get started on that, it's important to know that a great e-commerce site by itself does not mean success. The successful formula for e-commerce is a great site plus high-ROI promotion to get buyers to your site. To compare e-commerce to eBay, buyers are essentially what you are paying eBay for, so you should be prepared to pay for buyers on your own e-commerce site.

The top promotional vehicles for an e-commerce site are these:

- **Search engines/portals.** There are two strategies for promoting your e-commerce site via search engines such as Google, Yahoo!, MSN, and others. For algorithmic results, you can optimize your e-commerce site to show up high in the "free" results.

Chapter 7 Summary

Today most search engines also have a "paid-search" area, also known as sponsored links or listings. In these cases, you pay per click to be displayed when someone searches for various terms or keywords. When someone clicks a link in your ad and goes to your site, you pay the search engine company the cost per click. Then it's up to you to convert the visitor into a customer.

Sponsored listings are displayed using an auction-per-keyword system, such that the seller willing to pay the most on a per-click basis shows up first. You should experiment with paid search very carefully. Because millions of searches are performed each day, a simple mistake can be very costly. Although you can set up budgets, we have seen examples of sellers accidentally spending much more money than they anticipated.

- **Shopping engines.** At most portals, as well as on independent sites, many buyers use shopping engines to decide which e-commerce site to buy from. Outside of the portals (such as Yahoo! Shopping, Shop@AOL, MSN shopping, and others), there are independent popular shopping engines such as Shopping.com, mySimon, and PriceGrabber.com.

  With shopping engines, you pay per click. Logistically, you need to figure out how to get your SKUs (called your catalog) to the shopping engine so you will show up in their database of merchants. In shopping engines, you can typically change how much you are willing to pay only by category, not by keyword.

- **Affiliate programs.** Another successful promotional tool for e-commerce is an affiliate program. Basically, you agree to provide a revenue share to Web site owners who send buyers to you. This motivates Web site owners, called your affiliates, to promote your products and your e-commerce store on their sites. You can develop your own affiliate program or outsource it to one of several providers.

■ **E-mail newsletters.** Given the investment you will make to acquire online customers, one of the best ways to get the most from that investment is to provide a high-quality e-mail newsletter. Some of the most effective newsletters include useful information in addition to weekly or monthly specials.

In conclusion, there are numerous options out there; we highly recommend that you start to explore them as your business matures. If you want to dip your toe in the water, Amazon Marketplace and Yahoo! Stores are great, relatively safe, and easy places to get started.

If you want to jump in headfirst, building your own e-commerce site and experimenting with search engine marketing, shopping engines, affiliate programs, and e-mail newsletters will give you the best bang for your promotional buck.

Note that with each of these channels, you can optimize them using the same Five P's strategic framework we have been discussing for eBay. Product, price, promotion, placement, and performance are as relevant for Amazon.com, Yahoo!, and your e-commerce site as they are for eBay. The underlying details may change slightly, but you should still continue to use this methodology as you expand your business outside of eBay.

FOR MORE INFORMATION

Many of the following links may change, so check the book's blog at http://ebaystrategies.blogs.com for updates.

Chapter 7 Summary

Yahoo! Small Business Merchant Services

http://smallbusiness.yahoo.com/merchant/

Amazon.com Marketplace

http://www.amazon.com/exec/obidos/subst/misc/sell-your-stuff.html

Paid Search

Google AdWords program

http://adwords.google.com/

Overture—Paid search for Yahoo!, MSN, and others

http://www.overture.com

FindWhat—Paid search for Lycos and others

http://www.findwhat.com

Affiliate Programs

Commission Junction (CJ)—Affiliate program provider

http://www.commissionjunction.com

LinkShare—Affiliate program provider

http://www.linkshare.com

Shopping Engines

Yahoo! Shopping—Yahoo!'s shopping engine

http://shopping.yahoo.com

MSN Shopping

http://shopping.msn.com

Shop@AOL

Inside the AOL environment and at http://webcenter.shop.aol.com

Shopping.com—Top independent shopping engine

http://www.shopping.com

PriceGrabber.com—Another popular independent shopping engine

http://www.pricegrabber.com

mySimon

http://www.mysimon.com

Chapter 7 Summary

BizRate

http://www.bizrate.com

NexTag

http://www.nextag.com

E-mail Newsletter Management Providers

Roving

http://www.roving.com

Topica

http://www.topica.com

EXERCISES

1. Take your top five SKUs from eBay and research their ASPs on the top shopping engines and on Amazon.com. Do the SKUs sell for more or less on these venues?

2. Go to Google or Yahoo!'s search engine and see if you can find the same SKUs being sold via sponsored listings. What are they selling for? Could you do better?

3. Sign up for a free trial account with Google or Overture and research how much some of your top eBay keywords would cost in the paid-search engines. Are they more or less? Calculate what conversion rate you would need to have positive ROI for the clickthrough rate on each keyword/SKU pairing.

eBay

Performance

Placement · Product · Performance · Price · Promotion

The core of the strategic eBay framework: performance

As you may have noticed in the Five P's strategy framework diagrams shown so far, performance lives at the center, or the heart, of the framework. That's because if you do not measure the performance of the strategic changes you make to your eBay business, you won't know if the strategies are improving the business or driving it into the ground. Also, as the diagram illustrates, price, product, promotion, and placement are all interrelated. In other words, if you change one, the others change as well. The last *P* of the Five P's strategic framework, *performance,* enables you to document the changes you are making, and to see the impact across all parts of your eBay business.

In Chapter 2, we introduced the concept of eBay vitals. As you start to use the Five P's, it will be important to constantly measure your eBay vitals across each *P* (product, price, promotion, and placement), so you'll know exactly what changes to your eBay vitals you are causing by utilizing the Five P's framework.

In this chapter, we introduce the concept of *dashboards,* which is a technique we highly recommend for measuring your eBay performance.

10 USE AN EBAY DASHBOARD

To help you track your progress, we strongly recommend that you develop and maintain an *eBay dashboard.* An eBay dashboard provides a one-page "control center" report that gives you all of the critical information about your eBay business in an easy-to-see and easy-to-digest format. We use the term *dashboard* because, like the dashboard of a car, the eBay dashboard tells you how fast your business is going and if your business is overheating.

Also, instead of just a snapshot of the business, we recommend that the dashboard include several periods of data, so that you can measure the impact of strategic changes over a period of time.

Since the average eBay auction cycle is seven days, most sellers tend to think of their businesses in seven-day, or weeklong, chunks. We tend to recommend picking one day of the week (usually Sunday) and making that day the starting point of any time period you measure in a dashboard.

In fact, we recommend maintaining one to three dashboards, over these increasingly long time frames:

- **Weekly dashboard. The weekly dashboard shows the most recently completed week and the past three weeks, giving you four weeks of data, or about a month's worth.**

- **Monthly/quarterly dashboard. This dashboard measures the results of the most recently completed month as well as the past two months, for a quarter's worth of monthly results. This format will allow you to catch larger trends that you may not notice when looking at micro-periods such as a week or a month.**

- **Annual dashboard. The final dashboard we recommend is an annual dashboard. This should show either the last four quarters' worth of data or the last 12 months' worth of data. The annual dashboard will allow you to track your annual goals and enable you to make *year over year*** (frequently abbreviated as *y/y*) comparisons. With the annual report, you will be able to answer questions like the following:

- What was my conversion rate a year ago?

- How much has my GMS changed over the last year?

- Has my ASP increased or decreased over the year, and what's the trend?

For the purposes of this chapter, we focus on the shorter-term, weekly dashboard, but the basic concepts of the dashboards are all the same—only the time frames and date ranges vary.

eBay Dashboard Vital Signs

If you want to put together a one-page weekly dashboard that's the easiest to create and most impactful, we recommend minimally including the following:

- **Gross merchandise sales (GMS).** The revenue or gross sales, frequently known as GMS on eBay. GMS trends allow you to see from the widest perspective how your business is doing on the surface.

- **Units sold.** Units sold allows you to monitor the logistical activity of your business. You may need to hire additional help or lease a new facility when certain limits are met, so keeping track of this measure can be important for many eBay businesses.

- **Average sales price (ASP).** As previously discussed, average sales price varies depending on the product, or on the SKU mix. Decreases in ASP may not necessarily be bad for your business, but they are important to track and understand.

- **Conversion rate (CR).** The conversion rate is the ratio of sold items to listed items. Following this trend will alert you to any changes in the demand for your products. If you see a steep decrease, for example, you may want to look at all of the products you are selling and review the strategy being used to try to increase the SKU-level conversion rate as well as the macro-level conversion rate.

- **Margin.** Also known as profit, or the bottom line. We recommend a simple gross margin calculation here, where the margin is calculated as the GMS minus the costs of the products sold.

- **Feedback/customer service.** Your feedback rating represents the state of your customer service. We recommend tracking it closely. If a negative comment is received, your dashboard should specifically call that out, because it is a cause for concern and could indicate a customer service or logistics problem with your business.

- **Promotional/traffic trends.** From a promotional standpoint, one page doesn't give much room for information, so we recommend a big-picture view of promotion. The best indicator of promotional activity is traffic to your listings, to your About Me page, and to your eBay store (if you have one).

Here are other data you may want to consider including on your dashboard:

- **NPB rate.** If your eBay business has an NPB problem and you want to track it closely, you should add an NPB element to your dashboard.

- **eBay fees as percentage of sales (take rate).** Many sellers who see their eBay fees eat away at their margin keep a very close eye on their take rate. The conversion rate is a key factor in your take rate, which we've already recommended tracking. If eBay fees concern you, you may want to consider also tracking the take rate.

- **Shipping and handling income/margin.** As previously mentioned, many sellers rely on shipping and handling as a source of income and margin. If you fall into that camp, then you should definitely consider tracking the shipping and handling revenues and margin in your dashboard. Another metric you may want to track is the average shipping and handling income/margin per unit sold.

- **Average order value/items per order (AOV/IPO).** If you support multi-item consolidation per order, you may want to track the average order value and the items per order.

- **Attach rate.** If you support and rely on up-sells or cross-sells in your checkout, you should track and monitor the attach rate for your business, so you can work to increase it.

- **Average bids per listing.** Some sellers like to monitor bids per listing as a metric, so they can get a gut feel for the demand for their items.

- **Unique buyers acquired.** Occasionally, businesses will sell on eBay with the primary or secondary goal of customer acquisition. If this is your goal, you can track your progress by measuring the number of unique buyers acquired over a period of time. Usually this requires checking buyers against a customer relationship management (CRM) system.

Sample eBay Dashboard

Every eBay business is different. You should develop your
own dashboard to track *your* goals in a format that works
best for *you*. That being said, there are enough similarities
among businesses that we can give you a comprehensive
start on a generic dashboard, which you can customize for
your business.

The sample dashboard presented in the rest of the
chapter was created using Microsoft Excel and saved as an
Adobe Acrobat PDF file for optimal printing. The source
files are readily available at the book's blog and discussion
group, so you can use them to enter the data for your business and customize them to meet your needs.

Figure 8.1 shows the sample dashboard. As we go
through the sample dashboard, we will also provide some
analysis based on the sample data for our fictitious seller.

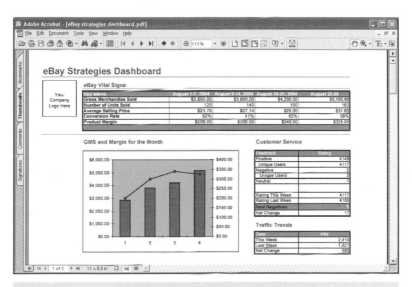

FIGURE 8.1   Sample *eBay*™ *Strategies* dashboard

EBAY VITAL SIGNS

In the sample report, the first section is called eBay Vital Signs. In this sample, we have chosen to track for the past four weeks the GMS, units sold, ASP, CR, and margin. A quick glance at this data in the sample shows you a great deal about this fictitious eBay business:

- GMS is trending up nicely. Over the last four weeks, we can quickly see that GMS has grown from $2,850 to $5,150 for the just-completed week (August 22–28 in this example).

- As you would expect with increasing GMS, the number of units sold is rising. Tracking units sold will help you plan for logistics. For example, in the sample report, the business has gone from shipping 120 units a week to 163 units. This business may be able to comfortably ship only 200 units a week; based on the trend over the last four weeks, that limit will be hit in two to four weeks if growth continues.

- The fictitious seller has been using the strategies in this book to increase the ASP, which has gone from $23.75 four weeks ago to $31.60 in the most current week.

- The conversion rate trend looks relatively healthy, except for the second period (August 8–14), when the conversion rate fell significantly from 52% to 41%. Fortunately, the CR recovered in the third week—most likely because the seller used the dashboard to see the drop and changed some promotions/product mix/pricing strategies to drive the conversion rate back up as soon as possible.

▪ **Product margin presents a challenge for this seller. The trend in the first three weeks was relatively positive, but margin in the last period (August 22–28) has actually decreased, while GMS and other eBay vital statistics went up. Thanks to the dashboard, this trend is easy to spot, and the seller has caught the negative trend quickly and has begun working on it for the next week.**

The eBay Vital Signs portion of the dashboard illustrates important trends that "at a glance" should show you the health of your business.

THE GMS AND MARGIN CHART

The chart on the bottom of the sample dashboard illustrates the same trends suggested by the data in the eBay Vital Signs section. Specifically, the bars in the chart represent the GMS, using the left-hand axis. The line graph illustrates the margin over four weeks, or a monthly period.

By glancing at this chart, you quickly see that the seller's GMS tracks well, but the margin is a concern, as already mentioned.

You know the adage that a picture is worth a thousand words. A picture like the GMS and margin chart can highlight trends in your business that you may not be able to see by looking at the numeric data. Plus, many people are more visual than analytical; the Product Margin row in the eBay Vital Signs section may not mean much to these folks, but the dip in margin shown on the chart jumps right off the page.

CUSTOMER SERVICE

The Customer Service section summarizes the week's feedback activity for the seller. In this example, the seller had an increase of 17 feedbacks. Unfortunately, a negative was submitted; it's highlighted in the report so the seller can remedy the situation. Additionally, the seller should make sure there are no other systemic problems with the business's logistics like the one that caused the negative feedback.

TRAFFIC TRENDS

The Traffic Trends section highlights any changes (positive or negative) in the amount of traffic to your listings, About Me page, and eBay Store over the last week. This summary information can alert you to changes that need further exploration.

THE POWER OF THE DASHBOARD

The dashboard gives you a single piece of paper containing the information you need to monitor your business and detect any positive or negative trends. Not only is the information nice to have, but it is also very actionable, as we have seen by analyzing the data in the sample dashboard.

More Dashboard Ideas

If you have the time or if your auction-management software (AMS) can automatically generate reports easily, we also recommend creating a one-page dashboard to measure the performance of the other four *P's*: product, price, promotion, and placement. These Five P's strategy framework dashboards will allow you to "peel the onion" and easily apply and measure the strategies outlined in this book. Doing so will give you a total of five pages—one for each of the Five P's. Once you have them, you won't believe you were ever able to run your business without them.

Another "best practice" we have seen is to use a three-hole punch on your reports each week and keep them in a simple three-ring binder. This way, when you want to go back five months and look at the performance of a certain SKU, pricing strategy, or promotional activity, you will have the information at your fingertips.

The rest of this chapter details additional dashboards you should consider, along with detailed samples of each.

The Product Dashboard

In Chapter 4, we introduced the strategic importance of product in your eBay business. As you go to source product or think about what to list next, wouldn't it be nice to have a one-page dashboard that shows the SKUs you are currently selling and their performance?

To hone your product strategy, you need to dig deeper than the eBay vitals shown on the "big-picture" eBay dashboard. On a per-SKU basis, a product dashboard should show the following:

- **GMS. By evaluating the GMS for each SKU, you can see what percentage each SKU contributes to your total GMS. This helps you identify your top SKUs, as well as the ones that contribute the least. You can then focus on the ones doing well or try to fix those that aren't—or both.**

- **CR. Understanding the CR on a SKU-by-SKU basis will let you determine if the product "turns" quickly and see how the SKU contributes to your overall CR. For example, if individual products fall below the overall CR for your entire business, you can focus on increasing their sell-through rate to bring up the entire metric.**

- **ASP.** By tracking the average selling price, you can calculate your blended margin by subtracting your cost on the item to figure out your absolute margin.

- **Margin.** It's very important to track margin at the SKU level, so that when you go to source more product, you have a crystal-clear understanding of what your most and least profitable products are. Obviously, you want to focus on sourcing higher-margin rather than lower-margin product.

- **Gross margin percentage.** As you dig into the profitability of your entire eBay business, one useful metric is the gross margin percentage on a SKU-by-SKU basis. While gross margin is the value of the item sold minus the cost you paid to acquire it, the gross margin percentage is the percentage of margin you make on the product—that is, the gross margin divided by the GMS for the SKU. For example, if you buy a product for $80 and sell it for $100, your gross margin is $20 and your gross margin percentage is 20%. In other words, what portion of the selling price was profit?

- **Traffic.** When you think about which products are hottest, you may find it useful to measure the amount of traffic your listings receive on a SKU-by-SKU basis.

- **eBay fees.** If you really want a crystal-clear margin picture, you may want to look at eBay fees (either absolute or as take rate) on a SKU-by-SKU basis, to see if any SKUs are generating abnormally high or low eBay fee situations for you.

- **NPB rate.** If NPBs are a large problem for your eBay business, you may want to track the percentage of NPBs on a SKU-by-SKU basis. This will help you identify any SKUs with abnormally high or low NPB rates and react accordingly.

This is the basic data that most sellers want to see. As you get used to using a product dashboard, you may want to customize it to include more promotional information, source information, or even data such as the number of bids per SKU. Some sellers also pull information from their inventory system so they can include data such as "inventory on hand," along with the eBay product performance data.

Once you are able to regularly see all of this strategic product information in a product dashboard, you will be amazed at how quickly and easily you can make important strategic product decisions that you previously made only by intuition.

A Sample Product Dashboard

Figure 8.2 shows a sample product dashboard that contains all of the basic elements we recommend.

The first section of the sample product dashboard is called Product Vital Signs and basically recaps some of the information from the main dashboard, such as:

- ASP

- GMS

- Conversion rate

- Margin

We recommend repeating these vital statistics on the product dashboard so that when you dig into each SKU's vitals, you can easily compare each SKU's stats to your overall business vitals.

PRODUCT DETAILS

The Product Details section of the product dashboard lists all of the SKUs sold over a period of time (the week of August 22, 2004, in this sample) and provides information on the SKU-level vital statistics for each SKU.

Product Dashboard

Product Vital Signs   Week of August 22, 2004

Total Units Sold	163
Average Selling Price	$31.60
Total Gross Merchandise Sold	$5,150.00
Conversion Rate	58%
Margin	$325.00

Product Details

Rank	SKU	Title	Listed	Sold	CR	GMS	GMS %	ASP	Margin	GM %	Avg Hits / Day
1	TEST1	Seben 1.25" Telescope	54	25	46%	$1,417.25	28%	$56.69	$119.24	8%	145
2	AUTO3	RMR Radar Detector Holder	30	30	100%	$367.50	7%	$12.25	$53.25	14%	3
3	MISC3	RZ500 Motorized Scooter	8	8	100%	$368.00	7%	$46.00	$25.22	7%	43
4	MISC4	Billiard Ball Set	27	13	48%	$389.87	8%	$29.99	$20.32	5%	44
5	AUTO2	MTX Thunder 100 200 Watt Amplifier	25	15	60%	$744.75	14%	$49.65	$17.00	2%	19
6	AUTO1	Garrett Twin TI04E Nitrous Pack	10	8	80%	$361.60	7%	$45.20	$17.00	5%	35
7	TEST3	Vintage Ruby Earrings	40	12	30%	$59.76	1%	$4.98	$15.68	26%	33
8	MISC2	RZ300 Motorized Scooter	8	6	75%	$192.00	4%	$32.00	$13.12	7%	45
9	CE3	Sony CFDG55 Portable Boom Box	10	8	80%	$155.44	3%	$19.43	$11.81	8%	170
10	TEST4	Kitchenaid Professional 525W 6Qt Blender	5	5	100%	$225.00	4%	$45.00	$10.21	5%	21
11	CE2	Kodak DX3215 1.3mp Digicam	15	10	67%	$487.60	9%	$48.76	$8.77	2%	200
12	CE1	Audiovox AVP7280 VHS player	17	2	12%	$59.90	1%	$29.95	$6.70	11%	3
13	TEST5	2.4 Ghz Wireless Baby monitor system	2	2	100%	$44.68	1%	$22.34	$2.82	6%	56
14	MISC1	RZ100 Motorized Scooter	8	4	50%	$92.00	2%	$23.00	$2.21	2%	22
15	TEST2	Intel PRO/100 Cardbus Mobile Adapter Type III	20	15	75%	$184.65	4%	$12.31	$1.65	1%	34
	Totals:		279	163	58%	$5,150.00		$31.60	$325.00	6%	872

FIGURE 8.2   Sample product dashboard

In the sample product dashboard, each SKU has the following information:

- **Rank.** The seller in this sample chose to rank his SKUs by the absolute margin.

- **SKU.** Many sellers assign their own SKU number to an item or perhaps use the manufacturer's system. In this example, the seller gives each SKU a unique identifier based on the product's category. For example, AUTO1 is an automotive product. The numbering system isn't clear, but it's probably just sequential, based on when the product was sourced. Thus, AUTO1 was sourced before AUTO2, and so on.

- **Title.** You may not be able to determine the nature of a SKU based on its SKU number. A brief title is included in the dashboard to let you know exactly what the SKU is.

- **Listed.** The number of times the SKU was listed over the course of the reporting period.

- **Sold.** Sold details the quantity of the SKU sold over the reporting period.

- **CR.** CR provides the conversion rate on a SKU-by-SKU basis for the reporting period.

- **GMS.** The amount of GMS the individual SKU generated over the reporting period.

- **ASP.** The average sales price for the SKU.

- **Margin.** The absolute gross margin generated by the SKU over the reporting period.

- **GM%.** The percentage of gross margin driven by the SKU.

- **Hits/day.** The average number of hits (unique views) received by the SKU over the reporting period.

Analyzing each column of the SKU report, we quickly make the following positive observations:

- The TEST1 SKU is very strong, because it performs above all of the eBay vitals for this business. For example, the TEST1 ASP is significantly higher than the average. Most important, TEST1's margin is relatively large, on both an absolute and a gross margin percentage basis.

- The MISC1, MISC2, and MISC3 SKUs are all motorized scooters that appear to have different model numbers (indicating different features). When compared, MISC3 (the RZ500) definitely performs the best, with the largest absolute margin, GM%, and ASP. The MISC1 SKU (RZ100) performs the worst, with below-average ASP and poor margin. MISC2 (RZ300) is in the middle.

- There's definitely a trend with this seller: AUTO and MISC SKUs perform better than CE and TEST SKUs (with the exception of the telescope, TEST1). The seller may want to focus on the AUTO category and on the MISC category. With the success of telescopes, we would recommend more exploration of that category as well.

Also, you may notice the following negative observations:

- The TEST2 SKU performs poorly. All of the SKU's vitals are lower than those for the entire business, except for CR. For example, the ASP, margin, and margin percentage are poor, and they bring these metrics down for the entire business. Based on limited information, it is most likely that the strategy for this SKU needs to be evaluated and given a week or two to improve. If it does not, the item should be liquidated and not sourced again.

- The CE1 SKU's conversion rate of 12% looks risky, because the eBay fees on this SKU alone (listed 17 and sold 2) destroy the entire $6.70 margin. Depending on the listing and pricing strategy, the seller is probably losing significantly on this SKU once eBay fees are taken into consideration.

- The TEST3 CR also appears to be lower than average. That being said, 30% isn't too much cause for alarm and can easily be improved by changing the listing/pricing strategy to try to "crank up" the velocity of the product. As we've seen with the price/velocity curve, this could decrease the ASP, but small changes probably will not have a negative impact. Plus, with this dashboard, a decrease in ASP for the SKU will immediately be noticeable in the next week's product dashboard.

- Given the poor performance of CE product, we recommend this seller turn his focus to sourcing other categories of product that appear to be performing better, such as AUTO.

These points represent just a handful of the observations you can find when you look at your business from a strategic product perspective.

Imagine how much smarter the seller will be with the product dashboard in hand the next time he goes to source product.

The Price Dashboard

In Chapter 5, we introduced the strategic concept of price and how it affects your eBay business. To manage how you price your items, we recommend you develop and maintain a price dashboard. We have found that most sellers make price decisions based on each individual SKU or category or classification, so a generic price dashboard should allow you to sort by any of these variables.

In fact, because you should look at price strategies on a SKU-by-SKU basis, many elements from the product dashboard shown previously can be reused in the price dashboard, such as the SKU number, Listed, Sold, CR, GMS, ASP, Margin, and Margin%.

The key *additional* elements we recommend are these:

- **Pricing Strategy.** To know how your current pricing strategy is doing, you will need to document what the strategy is.

- **Classification.** As mentioned in previous chapters, frequently you can decide pricing strategy based on the classification or class of a product. In Chapter 4, we introduced the concept of Class A, B, and C product—with Class A being the highest-margin product and Class C being "blow it out" product.

- **Previous ASP.** In your price dashboard, not only do you need to see the latest period's pricing/ASP information, but also the previous period's data, so you can spot price trends compared to the last period(s).

- **ASP Change Percentage.** The percentage change in ASP (positive or negative) between the current period and the past period, expressed as a percentage.

Armed with this information for each SKU you carry, you can easily monitor your strategic pricing decisions, measure their success, and make improvements as you see any negative trends you want to reverse.

A Sample Price Dashboard

Figure 8.3 illustrates a sample price dashboard that provides all of the generic information recommended here.

The first section of the sample price dashboard, called Price Vital Signs, recaps the eBay vitals for units sold, ASP, GMS, and CR and highlights the change in the ASP from the last period (the previous week, in this example).

EBAY PRICE DETAILS

The eBay Price Details section of the sample price dashboard looks similar to the product dashboard, with the addition of the price-critical new columns recommended for price dashboards.

Price Dashboard

Price Vital Signs   Week of August 22, 2004

Total Units Sold	163
Average Selling Price	$31.60
Total Gross Merchandise Sold	$5,150.00
ASP change w/w	5%
Conversion Rate	58%

eBay Price Details

Rank	SKU	Pricing Strategy	Class	Listed	Sold	CR	GMS	ASP	Margin	Mrgn%	Prev ASP	Change
1	CE1	$1NR Dutch	C	17	2	12%	$59.90	$29.95	$6.70	11%	$14.95	100%
2	TEST3	$4NR w/ SCO @ $4	B	40	12	30%	$59.76	$4.98	$15.68	26%	$2.98	67%
3	AUTO1	$40 NR	A	10	8	80%	$361.60	$45.20	$17.00	5%	$32.50	39%
4	TEST1	Perception of scarcity	A	54	25	46%	$1,417.25	$56.69	$119.24	8%	$43.21	31%
5	TEST2	$9.99 NR	B	20	15	75%	$184.65	$12.31	$1.66	1%	$9.99	23%
6	AUTO2	SCO with $17 margin	A	25	15	60%	$744.75	$49.65	$17.00	2%	$40.97	21%
7	CE2	$40 NR w/ 4% margin SCO	B	15	10	67%	$487.60	$48.76	$8.77	2%	$40.76	20%
8	MISC1	$1NR	C	8	4	50%	$92.00	$23.00	$2.21	2%	$22.00	5%
9	TEST5	$1NR	C	2	2	100%	$44.68	$22.34	$2.82	6%	$21.45	4%
10	MISC2	$1NR	C	8	6	75%	$192.00	$32.00	$13.12	7%	$31.00	3%
11	MISC3	$1NR	C	8	8	100%	$368.00	$46.00	$25.22	7%	$45.00	2%
12	MISC4	$29.99 BIN	A	27	13	48%	$389.87	$29.99	$20.32	5%	$29.99	0%
13	TEST4	$1NR	C	5	5	100%	$225.00	$45.00	$10.21	5%	$65.00	-31%
14	CE3	$.99 NR	C	10	8	80%	$155.44	$19.43	$11.81	8%	$29.34	-34%
15	AUTO3	$.99 NR	B	30	30	100%	$367.50	$12.25	$53.25	14%	$24.23	-49%
	Totals:			279	163	58%	$5,150.00	$31.60	$325.00	6%	$ 30.22	5%

FIGURE 8.3   A sample price dashboard

The toughest column to generate and maintain automatically is the Pricing Strategy column. Most sellers keep track of this "by hand" and have their own shorthand to describe the pricing strategies they utilize. However, some advanced auction-management software may be able to allow you to select strategies and report against those strategies.

Our fictitious seller has chosen to rank the SKUs in the price dashboard by ASP improvement on the far right column, from most improved to least improved. The seller could just as easily have sorted by classification or margin or current ASP, depending on how he wanted to look at the data. In fact, we recommend sorting SKU-by-SKU data by several different columns so you can see any trends you may miss by sorting on a different column.

Reviewing the sample report, we quickly see the following:

- **With the CE1 SKU, the $1NR Dutch strategy has shown a 100% improvement in the ASP of the product. This is unusual and achievable only with considerable promotion. So most likely, this SKU has received the benefit of a Featured Plus! promotion or some eBay Keywords.**

  Let's assume that the seller used a $20 Featured Plus! on the SKU. Was this a wise investment? Your intuition may lead you to say "Yes" because the Featured Plus! and Dutch strategy doubled the ASP for this product. But when you look at the data, you see that the seller invested $20 for an absolute margin of $6.70, yielding a very negative return for the promotion.

- **The TEST4, CE3, and AUTO3 SKUs are experiencing rapidly decreasing ASP. As discussed in Chapter 5, this usually indicates either new competition, a change in the broader market, or the effect of your pricing strategy driving down the ASP by flooding the market with supply. Assuming we have a pricing strategy problem, the strategy on these three SKUs must immediately be altered if you want to move the**

ASP back in a positive trend. However, TEST4 and CE3 are marked as Class C products, so maybe the seller feels they should be liquidated rapidly. If that's the case, then velocity is more important than price, and the current strategy may be appropriate.

Given the data in this sample price dashboard, there are literally hundreds of other observations that could be made. Are you able to look at your pricing decisions in this kind of detail today? If not, we highly recommend starting and maintaining a price dashboard so you can make the most intelligent, well-informed pricing decisions possible.

The price dashboard will also allow you to experiment with some of the advanced pricing strategies introduced in Chapter 5 and to *measure* the performance to see what impact these strategies are having on your eBay business.

The Promotion Dashboard

In Chapter 6, we introduced the strategic concept of promotion and how it can extend the price/velocity curve for you. A promotional dashboard will allow you to track your ongoing promotions and their ROI. Because eBay provides numerous promotional opportunities, most sellers will have vastly different promotional dashboards. Some may prefer to look at "the big picture," and others may prefer to look at SKU-by-SKU promotional activities and results.

If you'll recall, on the main eBay dashboard, we recommended a section that showed the amount of traffic to your items and to your About Me page. For the promotional dashboard, we recommend tracking the following:

- **Total traffic.** The total traffic generated to your listings, your About Me page, and your eBay Store.

- **Top traffic sources.** The top sources, or referrals, for traffic to your items, About Me pages, and eBay Store pages.

- **Top search terms.** As mentioned in Chapter 6, one of the most important promotional considerations you make in any eBay business is choosing the keywords included in your auction titles. By tracking the top search terms generating hits to your items, you can make sure you are properly leveraging the 55 characters in your titles.

- **Traffic trend.** To see promotional trends, you may want to track the traffic to your items over the span of three to four periods and even put a chart of the traffic on your promotion dashboard.

- **Peak traffic time.** Your counter/auction-management software may be sophisticated enough to tell you the peak traffic time for the traffic that came to your listings and other pages over the last period. Going forward, you can use this information to time auction closings to occur at or around peak traffic times.

For a SKU-by-SKU promotional report, you may also want to include the following elements on a per-SKU basis:

- **SKU traffic (hits).** The traffic to all of the listings for each specific SKU.

- **SKU traffic change percentage.** The change in traffic week over week to all of the listings for the specific SKU, expressed as a percentage. For example, if traffic to all listings of a SKU in the current week is 1,000 and in the previous week it was 800, there is a 20% week-over-week improvement.

- **Top traffic source per SKU.** Tracking the top traffic source for each SKU will allow you to see trends of what is working and what isn't. For example, first you may notice a jump in ASP for a SKU, and then when you look at the promotion report, you see that a new top traffic source is driving the increase.

- **Top 1 to 4 search terms for each SKU.** Tracking the top search terms on each SKU will allow you to tightly optimize the titles for your SKUs for maximum promotional traffic from the eBay search engine.

- **SKU promotions.** If you are running any promotions such as Bold, Highlight, Gift Services, Featured Plus!, or SKU-targeted eBay Keywords, you should make a note similar to the pricing strategy note on the sample price dashboard.

- **Peak traffic time.** Your counter/auction-management software may be able to provide you with peak traffic times on a SKU-by-SKU basis.

N O T E

If you have an eBay Store, you can take advantage of eBay's recently introduced eBay Store traffic report. You can read about it and see samples here: http://pages.ebay.com/storefronts/traffic-reports.html

A Sample Promotion Dashboard

In our experience, sellers highly customize their promotion dashboard. The sample dashboard introduced in Figure 8.4 provides a generic promotion dashboard that can serve as a starting point for further customization.

First, the sample promotion dashboard repeats the top-level traffic information that was also presented on the eBay performance dashboard: total traffic, previous week's traffic, and the change over the last period.

Next, the Top Traffic Sources table reports the top eight sources of traffic and their percentage of total. For this

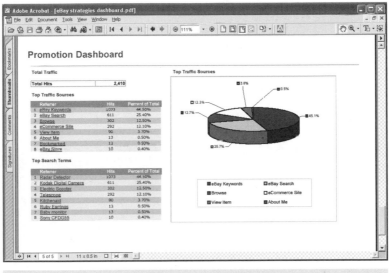

FIGURE 8.4 A sample promotion dashboard

seller, the top three referrers are eBay Keywords, the eBay search engine, and browsing, which represent more than 80% of the traffic.

The pie chart on the right side shows the same data in pie format, which helps you see graphically the percentages, or slices of the pie, that each traffic source represents.

Both the Top Traffic Sources table and the pie chart enable you to quickly see the top-performing promotions as well as the laggards, so you can focus on fixing the laggards and continuing to improve on promotions that are already working well for your business.

Finally, at the bottom of the sample promotion dashboard is a table that details the top eight search terms for the week. The Top Search Terms table gives you critical information on the most popular search terms, so you can optimize your auction titles appropriately. In addition to optimizing your titles, the top search terms can be used in an eBay Keywords promotional campaign.

Also, the Top Search Terms report indicates demand for various products and categories you carry. For example, in the sample promotion dashboard, there is clearly significant search activity for "Radar Detector," "Kodak Digital Camera," and "Electric Scooter," which, after further research, may indicate strong demand in the marketplace for products in these categories. Because the search terms are most likely competitive, you might want to consider using eBay Keywords banners for the terms, as well as setting up listing upgrades.

The Placement Dashboard

Finally, we recommend that you develop and maintain a placement dashboard, especially if you sell in multiple online channels in addition to eBay. The previous dashboards we've discussed have assumed the fictitious business is eBay only. We've saved other channels for the placement dashboard.

Your placement dashboard will vary based on the channels you support. For example, if you sell only on eBay, then you may not need a placement dashboard. However, if you do support multiple online channels, you'll need to measure the performance of those channels as closely as you measure the eBay performance.

First, in your placement dashboard you should report on the total vitals for all of your channels together, such as GMS, ASP, conversion rate, and combined channel costs/take rates for all your channels.

Next, on a channel-by-channel basis, your placement dashboard should show the vitals for each channel in detail.

Depending on how many systems you use to manage your various channels, it may require some extra work to get the data for each channel into a unified report, but you won't be able to see the true picture of your business until you do.

A Sample Placement Dashboard

A sample placement dashboard is provided in Figure 8.5. The sample placement dashboard has two major sections. The first section is Placement Vital Signs—All Channels, a complete summary of activity across all channels:

- **Total items posted.** The total items posted/listed to all channels.
- **Total items sold.** The total number of units sold across all channels.
- **Total items active.** The number of active items available on all channels.
- **Success percentage.** The conversion rate across all channels.
- **Sold as BIN.** The percentage of items sold at a fixed price rather than at a dynamic price.
- **ASP.** The average sales price for items on all channels.

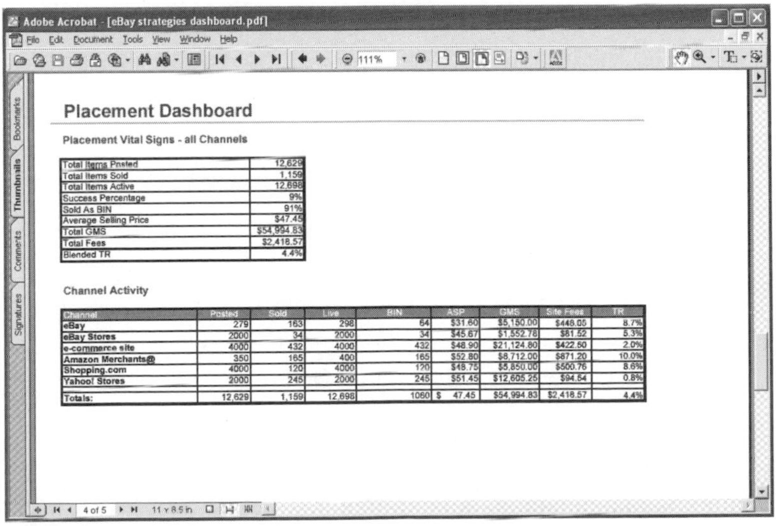

Placement Dashboard

Placement Vital Signs - all Channels

Total Items Posted	12,629
Total Items Sold	1,159
Total Items Active	12,698
Success Percentage	9%
Sold As BIN	91%
Average Selling Price	$47.45
Total GMS	$54,994.83
Total Fees	$2,418.57
Blended TR	4.4%

Channel Activity

Channel	Posted	Sold	Live	BIN	ASP	GMS	Site Fees	TR
eBay	279	163	298	64	$31.60	$5,150.00	$448.05	8.7%
eBay Stores	2000	34	2000	34	$45.67	$1,552.78	$81.52	5.3%
e-commerce site	4000	432	4000	432	$48.90	$21,124.80	$422.50	2.0%
Amazon Merchants@	350	165	400	165	$52.80	$8,712.00	$871.20	10.0%
Shopping.com	4000	120	4000	120	$48.75	$5,850.00	$500.76	8.6%
Yahoo! Stores	2000	245	2000	245	$51.45	$12,605.25	$94.54	0.8%
Totals:	12,629	1,159	12,698	1060	$ 47.45	$54,994.83	$2,418.57	4.4%

FIGURE 8.5 A sample placement dashboard

- **GMS.** The total sales/gross merchandise sales for all channels.

- **Fees.** The total channel/marketplace fees for all channels.

- **Blended TR.** The take rate, or fees as a percentage of GMS, across all channels.

Second is the Channel Activity portion of the report, where the following information for each channel is detailed:

- **Posted.** Items posted to the specific channel.

- **Sold.** Units sold on the channel.

- **Live.** Listings that are live on all channels (usually the same as SKUs except on eBay).

- **BIN.** Percentage of sales that are fixed price or buy-it-now rather than auction/dynamic price.

- **ASP.** Average sales price for the channel.

- **GMS.** GMS contribution for the channel.

- **% GMS.** The percentage of GMS attributable to the specific channel.

- **Site fees.** The fees charged by the site over the period.

- **TR.** The take rate for the channel, or fees as a percentage of GMS for the channel.

As you'll see in the sample report, when you're able to look at the performance of your business across channels, many observations can be made. For example, in the sample report, notice the following:

- **For this seller, the e-commerce channel drives substantial GMS at one of the lowest take rates of all channels.**

- **At 10%, the Amazon.com channel is one of the most expensive, but it also exhibits an ASP that is more than 10% higher** than the lowest-ASP channel. So, while the Amazon.com channel may appear to be the most expensive, it is likely the most profitable in this example. Note that Amazon.com does not charge listing fees.

- Shopping.com is only 11% of GMS, but it delivers a solid ASP at a relatively low take rate. Based on these results, the seller may want to consider increasing the focus on this channel to raise its percentage of the mix.

- Given the lower percentages on eBay, the seller may want to implement a placement strategy that places product first on Amazon.com or Yahoo! Stores for a period of time, next on their e-commerce site (promoting through Shopping.com), and finally on eBay. With the higher conversion rate for Amazon.com, we would recommend that channel first, with the information given. However, if the seller had a product/price report for each channel, he would be able to look at which SKUs convert best on which channel (and find the highest ASP per channel) and target product placement accordingly.

Performance Conclusions

As you have seen by studying the five recommended dashboards and samples presented in this chapter, a little up-front effort and weekly maintenance allows you to monitor the performance of your business with a relatively simple five-page report.

Once you have your dashboards, you will be able to quickly analyze them and create a weekly task list of product to liquidate, accelerate, and source; pricing strategies to improve; promotions to start/stop; and channels on which to place your products.

As you become familiar with the Five P's framework and start to leverage it to grow your business, you will find the dashboards essential to achieving your goals.

JustDeals.com

Seller: justdeals.com (87956 ⭐) me

Over the years, we've worked with literally thousands of sellers. Never have we met a seller that tracks their performance and works to improve it as aggressively as JustDeals.com. Given the size and complexity of their business, the performance measuring and enhancing systems they have built are very impressive.

eBay Vitals

- **GMS:** More than $200,000 per month on eBay alone; more than double that on other channels

- **ASP:** $20–$30

- **CR:** 70–75%

- **Feedback:** 97.6%

- Sells more than 15,000 items per month on eBay alone

Background

Based in Hayward, California, JustDeals started in the mid-1990s as primarily a wholesale business. In 1997, they listed their first item on eBay as an experiment. After they realized their returns selling on eBay were substantially higher than their wholesale business, they started to grow their eBay business significantly.

To continue growing, JustDeals.com opened a Yahoo! Store at JustDeals.com that does very well for them. Additionally, Just-Deals.com leverages these additional promotions and channels:

- **Amazon Marketplace.** JustDeals.com has a very active Amazon Marketplace presence.

- **Affiliate program.** To promote their Yahoo! Store, JustDeals.com has a very popular affiliate program, through which they syndicate specials on a weekly/monthly basis.

- **Search engine marketing/optimization.** JustDeals.com also promotes their Yahoo! Store by optimizing it for algorithmic search indexing and using paid-search to heavily promote their store.

- **Shopping engines.** JustDeals.com enjoys substantial traffic to their Yahoo! Store from shopping engines such as Yahoo! Shopping and Shopping.com.

- **eBay Store.** JustDeals.com also maintains an eBay Store, which they use for up-sells and other additional sales from eBay customers.

Today, JustDeals.com employs more than 25 people to keep their business humming, shipping out more than a thousand packages a day.

Figure 8.6 shows JustDeals.com's About Me page, Figure 8.7 shows one of JustDeals.com's popular items for sale on eBay, and Figure 8.8 illustrates the JustDeals.com Yahoo! Store.

JustDeals.com and Performance

Since switching in 1997 from a business-to-business wholesale model to a business-to-consumer model, JustDeals.com has focused on constantly and relentlessly improving the performance of their business. Over the years, JustDeals.com has invested substantial resources into a custom CRM system, as well as a complex reporting system.

The CRM system allows JustDeals.com to track customer acquisitions across channels, which they measure closely. In addition to counting which channels acquire the most customers, the Just-Deals.com CRM system allows them to track which customers are

FIGURE 8.6   JustDeals.com's About Me page

FIGURE 8.7   One of JustDeals.com's items for sale on eBay

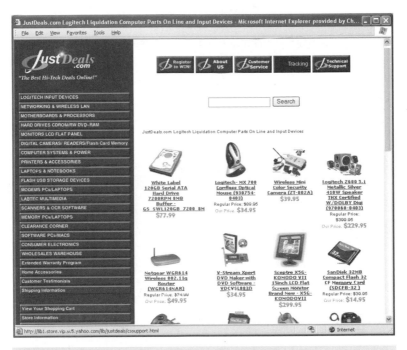

FIGURE 8.8   JustDeals.com's Yahoo! Store

most active. For example, they are able to measure the value of a customer acquired through the Google paid-search program as compared to a customer acquired by selling on eBay.

JustDeals.com uses an advanced auction-management system that provides them with the following:

- **eBay performance dashboard.** The eBay performance dashboard allows JustDeals.com to see on a single page a snapshot of their eBay business, as well as important trends over the last four weeks. JustDeals.com also analyzes the business on a monthly, quarterly, and annual basis.

- **Product dashboard.** The product dashboard allows JustDeals.com to measure how their SKUs are performing on eBay. JustDeals.com has so many SKUs, they are not able to fit on one page, but the reports are in Excel, so Just-Deals.com can sort them and analyze them dynamically.

In addition to using the product dashboard to decide product/price strategy, JustDeals.com uses the performance of products to determine what SKUs to source and in what quantity. As you can imagine, selling 15,000 units a month requires JustDeals.com to be very smart—and aggressive—about sourcing product.

- **Promotion dashboard.** The promotion dashboard allows JustDeals.com to measure how much traffic comes to all of their listings, their eBay Store, and their About Me page. They also carefully follow top search terms and use them in their listing titles.

In addition to the dashboards generated by their AMS, JustDeals.com imports all of the eBay sales information from their dashboards and other reports into their own reporting database. This database stores all of the information for non-eBay channels. Once the data has been unified in one database, JustDeals.com is able to run complex reports, including:

- **Placement report.** The placement report is similar to the placement dashboard introduced in this chapter.

- **Detailed SKU reports.** For every SKU they sell, JustDeals.com is able to explore a complete sales history of that SKU and slice and dice the data by channel. Armed with this information, they can easily determine the best plan for selling any SKU.

- **Detailed channel reports.** Beyond the placement report, JustDeals.com has created Five P's-style reports for every channel. So they are able to measure price per SKU across every channel, for example.

Thanks to the complete picture of their performance not only on eBay, but also across all channels, JustDeals.com is able to make extremely intelligent decisions throughout their enterprise. From sourcing product to pricing strategy, promotions, and placement,

JustDeals.com makes decisions based on closely watched performance and then measures the outcome of those decisions.

For example, JustDeals.com knows *when* they source a product exactly what channel they will start it on, the expected ASP, margin, and conversion rate, and the promotional plan for the SKU.

The time and effort invested by JustDeals.com to constantly improve their metrics and performance measuring tools has paid off handsomely for the company, allowing them to scale to a very impressive size in a short amount of time.

Other Strategies of Interest

On eBay, JustDeals.com leverages most of the promotional tools at their disposal. In addition to being a large eBay Keywords user, JustDeals.com utilizes many promotional strategies already discussed, such as Featured Plus!, heavily optimized titles, and carefully selected and measured listing upgrades.

Another interesting promotion from which JustDeals.com has seen a huge return—in positive feedback and in return customers (measured by their CRM system)—is a 30-day guarantee on most items. Some customers do abuse the system, but the percentage is relatively small, and JustDeals.com more than makes up for the cost of the program in increased bids, because buyers view their transaction to be very low risk.

One "best practice" JustDeals.com discovered early on for high feedback and a great customer experience is rapid shipping. In most cases, when you order from JustDeals.com, your order goes out within 12 hours. Customer expectations on eBay are very high, and JustDeals.com tends to exceed those expectations.

To get orders out rapidly and in huge volumes, JustDeals.com has implemented their own sophisticated shipping engine that takes orders from their AMS and other channels and routes them to the proper part of their warehouse for fulfillment.

Chapter 8 Summary

Dashboard—A one-page report that, like the dashboard of a car, gives you all the information you need to drive your eBay business.

KEY CONCEPTS

In this chapter, we introduced the fifth and final *P* of the Five P's strategic framework: performance. As illustrated in the Five P's strategic framework diagram that appears throughout the book, performance is at the heart of the strategy. Performance occupies the center of the framework because without the ability and discipline to measure your performance, you will never know if your attempts at any of the strategies outlined in this book have had a huge impact, a negative impact, or no impact at all. Therefore, the last and most important strategy is measuring and understanding the performance of your eBay business.

The eBay dashboard presents in one page, in an easy-to-read and easy-to-understand format, a snapshot of the most important vital signs for your business, including gross merchandise sales, average sales price, conversion rate, and margin.

The most effective eBay dashboard not only captures the vital signs, but also shows a trend over several periods of time. We recommend tracking the last four weeks of data (about a month's worth) so you can see short-term and long-term trends. Additionally, you may want to consider tracking the last three months' worth of data (a quarterly view) and the last 12 months' or four quarters' worth of data (an annual view).

Chapter 8 Summary

Figure 8.1 introduced a sample eBay dashboard that you can download at the book's blog or at its discussion group:

http://ebaystrategies.blogs.com

http://groups.ebay.com/forum.jspa?forumID=100006604

Four more dashboards were recommended for those who really want to track the complete performance of their eBay business and implement the Five P's strategic framework introduced in this book:

- **Product dashboard.** The product dashboard allows you to see the vital statistics for every SKU, such as the SKU's average sales price, conversion rate, and margin. Based on this information, you can make smarter sourcing decisions and develop better product sales strategies.

- **Price dashboard.** Like the product dashboard, the price dashboard presents information for every SKU. Instead of product information, the price dashboard presents the pricing strategy and pricing results for the SKU. This information allows you to measure the impact your price strategies are having on your business.

- **Promotion dashboard.** The promotion dashboard illustrates the impact your promotional activities are having on your business by showing the increase in traffic. You can also optionally look at promotion on a SKU-by-SKU basis. Additionally, we recommend tracking the top search terms so you can use the information in eBay Keywords and to optimize the titles of your listings.

Chapter 8 Summary

- **Placement dashboard. For eBay businesses that sell on multiple channels in addition to eBay, a placement dashboard will allow you to see how the various channels are performing. Important metrics for the placement dashboard are each channel's gross merchandise sales, average sales price, conversion rate, marketplace fees, and take rate.**

In addition to the sample for the eBay dashboard, samples for the other four dashboards are available at the book's blog and discussion forum.

EXERCISES

1. Put together an eBay dashboard for the last four weeks. What positive trends do you see? What negative trends do you notice? What actions can you take to enhance the positive trends and improve the negative trends?

2. What is your top-performing SKU? How do you measure that?

3. What channel works best for your business? Why? Which metrics do you use to measure the success of a channel?

4. What promotions that you utilize have the most impact?

5. What is the most effective pricing strategy you use?

Putting the Five P's to Work

Placement

Product

Performance

Promotion

Price

The strategic eBay framework

Now that we've covered each component of the Five P's framework in detail with case studies, we want to bring the discussion full circle and show a complete picture of a seller that used the entire framework to improve their eBay business dramatically over the last year.

Seller: urbanimport.com (1267 ☆) 🏆Power Seller me

If UrbanImport.com sounds familiar to you, that's because it's the business started by Michael, the high school student introduced in Chapter 1.

eBay Vitals

- GMS: **$20,000 per month on eBay; more than double that when counting other channels**

- ASP: **$50+**

- CR: **70–75%**

- Feedback: **99.0%**

As you may recall from Chapter 1, UrbanImport.com sells primarily auto parts. When I first met Michael in early 2003, the GMS for UrbanImport.com was in the range of only $2,000 to $4,000 per month, and Michael had the lofty goal of getting to $100,000 per month. At the time of this writing, UrbanImport.com is closing in on their goal at $40,000 per month, with $60,000 per month in sight, and they have three to five employees on staff.

Michael was able to achieve this 10× (1000%) year-over-year growth by following the Five P's framework outlined in this book, which allowed him to stay focused on the strategic decisions that have the most impact on his business.

In each of the following sections, we detail how Urban-Import.com strategically leveraged each component of the Five P's framework.

Product

As mentioned in Chapter 1, Michael started Urban-Import.com by selling race car seats in the Auto Parts category. Once he felt he had gone as far as possible with the race car seats, he stayed in the general category of Performance Auto Parts but started experimenting outside of seats in many other subcategories.

For a product strategy, UrbanImport.com decided to focus on their core customer: the performance car enthusiast. Over the last year they have experimented with hundreds, if not thousands, of different products in this category, with the goal of increasing the average order value (AOV) and lifetime value of the lucrative customer following they have built. In addition to AOV, with large items, UrbanImport.com realized they could both save the customer money and increase their margin by throwing in lots of other items with an order of a larger item. The metric used to track this is items per order or IPO.

Race car seats have a very large ASP: typically around $150 per seat (or $300 for a pair). As well as expanding selection and increasing AOV, Michael wanted to keep his ASP above $100—and increase it if possible. The top new categories that UrbanImport.com expanded into are these:

- **Performance enhancers. As the name suggests, the top goal for performance car enthusiasts is to increase the performance of their vehicle. UrbanImport.com helps their customers achieve this goal with high-end "kits," such as nitrous-oxide kits, performance computer chips, and more.**

- **Interior accessories. In addition to working on their engine and the exterior look of their car, performance car enthusiasts also work to customize the interiors of their vehicles. UrbanImport.com has gone very wide in this category, providing custom gearshift knobs, seats, custom pedals, shoulder pads, and complete interior packages.**

- **Exhaust systems.** Michael found that one of the highest-ticket items that performance car enthusiasts purchase is their exhaust system. Not only do his customers want their car to *be* fast, but they also want it to *sound* fast. Exhaust systems have a very high ASP, so they make a great new high-end product line for urbanimport.com

- **Head, tail, and running lights.** Another highly customizable area of any high-performance vehicle are the headlights and taillights. Over the last year, UrbanImport.com has added a significant selection of all of these options. Though the ASP on these products is lower than the target ASP, they are mostly "add-on" purchases with a larger item.

- **Wheels.** In addition to spending large amounts on performance kits and exterior and interior enhancers, performance car enthusiasts' next large purchase is typically a decorative and a utilitarian set of wheels. The ASP on wheels is huge, ranging from $100 to $175 *each* or $400 to $700-plus for a set of four.

- **Electronics.** UrbanImport.com also offers some electronics lines, targeted toward the performance car enthusiast.

- **Accessories.** UrbanImport.com also experimented and had success with smaller accessories that are typically $20 or less. Items such as special wiring kits, emblems, gauges, and so on don't drive the ASP, but they do dramatically increase the AOV metric and the number of items per order (IPO). Also, customers feel like they are getting a great deal if the shipping they have paid on a larger item allows them to get a smaller accessory for little or no extra shipping charges.

- **Videos.** When visiting some of the top performance auto retail brick-and-mortar stores, Michael realized that many offered both informative and entertaining videos for performance car enthusiasts. These videos were a strong draw for younger customers. Though the younger enthusiasts aren't in a position to spend much on their cars, getting them into the store when they are 14 or 15 turns them into very lucrative customers when they are in their best spending years, between 16 and 20. UrbanImport.com now offers videos and has found them to be a great customer acquisition vehicle, as well as a good accessory/add-on.

Michael's product strategy has been very effective and one of the primary drivers of UrbanImport.com's growth. In addition to maintaining and growing the ASP, the expanded product line has substantially increased the revenue per customer. For example, it's typical for a customer to be lured into UrbanImport.com's business on eBay by buying an "anchor item" such as a performance kit, exhaust system, set of wheels, or a set of seats. Once the customer has the anchor item, he tends to add on smaller items, such as a light kit, an interior upgrade, or a video.

This product strategy has increased all metrics substantially. For example, while the ASP has actually decreased some, the AOV has more than doubled, and the IPO is one of the largest we have seen for an eBay business. Another metric previously mentioned is attach rate, which is the percentage of orders/sales that result in an add-on/up-sell. UrbanImport.com enjoys an unusually large attach rate, on a par with a digital camera seller, but very unusual for an auto parts seller.

Sourcing

As recommended in Chapter 4, UrbanImport.com focuses a great deal on their sourcing strategy as part of their overall product strategy. For example, they have secured many exclusive distribution deals, and as sales have increased, they have actually traveled far abroad to locate products and introduce them exclusively to UrbanImport.com's U.S. customer base.

UrbanImport.com carefully measures the success of every product and uses that data to make every sourcing decision.

Product Life Cycle

Based on the UrbanImport.com eBay sales report, they have focused on selling primarily end-of-life product, as well as items they can sell at 30 to 50% off retail and still make margin. Other products that are in season are sold on different channels.

Price

UrbanImport.com's pricing strategy favors margin versus velocity. The eBay pricing strategy involves classifying the products into two classes:

- **Margin product:** product that has defined margin targets

- **Liquidation product:** product that has been on hand for a long period of time and needs to be moved rapidly, regardless of margin

The bulk of the UrbanImport.com product mix falls into the "margin product" category. The strategy is to start the bidding at a formula of cost-plus-margin, with a BIN that gives a great deal but is higher than the starting bid amount, to draw in convenience buyers.

About 10% of the UrbanImport.com product makes it to the "liquidation product" class. UrbanImport.com auctions that product starting with much lower starting bids (sometimes below cost) to focus on velocity rather than yield.

Promotion

Michael keeps close tabs on the top keywords for the eBay Motors Parts and Accessories category and makes sure to target those top keywords in the UrbanImport.com descriptions, being careful to maximize the 55 characters available.

UrbanImport.com has found that in the high-performance auto parts category, listing upgrades are not necessary to drive sales. Given the visual nature of their products, UrbanImport.com does use the Gallery listing upgrade on all listings.

From a brand-building perspective, UrbanImport.com's feedback speaks for itself, but they have also created a well-recognized and memorable brand on eBay.

Figure 9.1 illustrates a typical UrbanImport.com listing that shows their branding.

On top of the "best practices" described in Chapter 6, UrbanImport.com has created a couple of promotions of interest:

- **Free stickers.** Trendy, cutting-edge stickers are appealing to the performance auto audience, so UrbanImport.com lets every customer choose a specified color sticker. Performance car enthusiasts also tend to hang out in groups and clubs. Since the sticker says "UrbanImport.com," it's not only a nice perk for customers, it's also free advertising for UrbanImport.com!

FIGURE 9.1   A sample of UrbanImport.com's eBay branding

- **Gift certificates.** "Dad, I *really* want a new set of tires for my car for Christmas!" UrbanImport.com realized that many parents looking for a gift for their teenage son or daughter who is a performance car enthusiast would be interested in buying gift certificates. So now they sell them. In the 2003 holiday season, the gift certificates drove substantial revenue for UrbanImport.com.

- **Contact us.** Performance car enthusiasts usually have lots of questions about the items they are looking to buy. Does it work with their make and model? Are there other important specifications? To encourage customer contact and alleviate any concerns before purchasing, UrbanImport.com publishes three ways for prospective customers to contact them:

  - **E-mail.** UrbanImport.com clearly publishes their e-mail address in all listings and encourages customers to use it.

- **IM.** Also, UrbanImport.com publishes AOL Instant Messenger contact information and encourages prospects to contact them if they have questions.

- **Phone.** Finally, UrbanImport.com publishes their phone number and encourages calls during business hours.

Besides inviting prospective buyers to ask questions, publishing the contact information sets prospective customers at ease, most of whom are looking to spend more than $100. Being accessible makes it clear that UrbanImport.com has excellent customer service.

Placement

UrbanImport.com has a multifaceted placement strategy. First, on eBay they constantly measure the peak traffic times for each SKU and schedule the auctions to end during those individual peak traffic times.

Additionally, within eBay's Parts and Accessories category on eBay Motors, there are literally hundreds of categories where items can be placed. UrbanImport.com carefully researches the correct category and measures the results of tests in a variety of categories to determine the highest browser-trafficked category for each SKU.

Other Channels

In addition to eBay, UrbanImport.com has experimented with a variety of alternative online channels for their products. The most successful additional channel has been a Yahoo! Store hosted at http://www.urbanimport.com. See Figure 9.2. By creating this store, heavily promoting it, and

FIGURE 9.2   UrbanImport.com's Yahoo! Store

telling existing customers about it, UrbanImport.com has more than doubled their sales, basically creating a new channel that is as large as or even larger than eBay in some months.

UrbanImport.com promotes their Yahoo! e-commerce store by making the listings available on Yahoo! Shopping and other search engines. Additionally, UrbanImport.com judiciously uses paid-search and other top Internet promotional techniques to drive interest in their Yahoo! Store e-commerce site.

In the last month, UrbanImport.com has moved into a mixed retail/warehouse facility and added the additional channel of a retail store. Now online buyers have the option of coming to the retail facility to pick up products and avoid shipping fees (and potentially buying more products while in the store).

Performance

A 10× increase in revenue doesn't happen without a huge amount of effort, thoughtful strategy development, and careful measurement of the strategies being tested. It should come as no surprise that UrbanImport.com has implemented weekly reports similar to the five dashboards introduced in this book:

- **Overall report.** This report highlights the key metrics for the entire UrbanImport.com business and allows Michael to see the "big picture." The reports capture not only the previous week's worth of data, but also the trends for the quarter and the year.

- **Price/product report.** This report lists every SKU sold over a period, cost, price achieved, margin, AOV, IPO, and pricing strategy/classification. UrbanImport.com uses the price/product report to drive pricing going forward and to make sourcing/product mix decisions.

- **Marketplace report.** The marketplace report combines information from UrbanImport.com's Yahoo! Store, eBay sales, and retail operations to show the performance of each channel.

- **Promotion report.** The final report allows UrbanImport.com to track the amount and source of all traffic to both their eBay listings and Yahoo! Store. Based on this information, UrbanImport.com allocates their marketing budget between a variety of options.

Conclusion

By following the Five P's framework and focusing on the product, price, promotion, and placement strategies outlined in this book, UrbanImport.com was able to take significant strides toward the goal of being a million-dollar-a-year eBay business. Over the course of a year, they were able to grow their monthly revenues from $4,000 to $40,000—a factor of ten.

By continuing to improve their strategies, we're confident that UrbanImport.com will reach the million-dollar run rate of $84,000 per month in the next 6 to 12 months.

The Ten eBay Strategies

1 Know Your Critical eBay Vitals

L ike a patient at a hospital, your eBay business has "vital signs" that help you determine its health. Knowing the current vital signs and trends at a glance gives you a feeling for how your business is doing and the areas that might need improvement. The critical eBay vitals are these:

- **Gross merchandise sales (GMS).** The amount of sales you make over a period of time in your eBay business. In non-eBay businesses, this is typically called "revenue" or "income" or "gross sales." eBay uses the term *GMS* to report its own business to Wall Street, and most eBay sellers have adopted the same terminology, for consistency.

    If a seller sells 1,000 items at an average price of $50 over the course of a month, the seller's GMS is 1,000 × $50 = $50,000 for the month.

    Some sellers adjust their GMS downward based on non-paying bidders (NPBs), also known as unpaid items (UPI). eBay generates unpaid items when a winning bidder does not pay for the transaction and the seller gets no revenue. For some sellers, this amount is large enough that they subtract the sum of NPBs from GMS.

- **Average sales price (ASP).** An eBay business's average sales price is the measure of the average price for which you are selling your inventory over a period of time. ASP is calculated by dividing the GMS over time.

    If a seller's GMS over the course of a month is $25,000, and 300 items were sold, the ASP is $25,000 ÷ 300 = $83.33.

- **Conversion rate (CR).** On eBay, you list (or post) items for a period of time (1, 3, 5, 7, or 10 days). At the end of that time period, a percentage of those listings will result in a buyer, and a percentage will not. The percentage resulting in buyers is the conversion rate.

- **Margin.** Margin, also known as profit, is the amount of cash generated from your eBay business over a period of time, once all costs have been taken into account.

By measuring and monitoring the trends in these four vital signs, you will be able to get a feel for where your business is going and the impact your strategic decisions have on it—positive and negative.

Set Your Strategic Goals

2

Once you have a handle on your eBay vitals, you can use them to set a strategic goal for your business. The best strategic goal should include a time frame and specific targets for each critical eBay vital sign. For example, you may have a relative goal, such as increasing your GMS 10% over the next year. Or you may have a more absolute goal, such as building a million-dollar-a-year business in GMS. In addition to GMS goals, you may have a margin goal. Goals for ASP and CR are useful, but they typically are secondary to GMS and margin goals.

Once you have established a GMS or margin goal, you will be able to calculate ASP and CR goals that support the GMS/margin goal. Also, if you have a time frame associated with your strategic goal (such as a year or six months), you can break the larger goal time frame into smaller, easier to manage, subgoals.

A spreadsheet that calculates a one-year plan based on your current eBay vitals and your goals is provided at the book's blog:

http://ebaystrategies.blogs.com

3

Understand and Leverage the eBay Sweet Spots

Most products go through a well-defined product life cycle (although collectibles is an exception). Figure A.1 illustrates the typical product life cycle, which has four segments:

- **Introduction.** When products are first released to market. In this portion of the life cycle, hot products have more demand than supply. Also, when new products are introduced, it typically causes existing in-season retail products to head toward the end-of-life phase.

- **In-season retail.** The bulk of a product's sales come from the in-season retail portion of the product life cycle. These are the kinds of products you will find readily available in your local retail stores for "full price."

- **End of life.** Once a newer technology or replacement product is introduced, the current in-season products hit end-of-life status. Usually at the beginning of the end-of-life phase, these products flood the market. Later in the end-of-life phase, the products become scarcer and represent more of an opportunity.

- **Liquidation.** After end-of-life product is pushed out via price discounts, whatever is left is classified as liquidation product and is usually sold in bulk to liquidators.

Figure A.1 also shows that products in the introduction, end-of-life (toward the back half of this phase), and liquidation phases are "sweet spots" for eBay. Because eBay buyers are typically looking for deals in the range of 30 to 50% off retail or hot items they can't get anywhere else, the sweet spots of the product life cycle generate the best results.

eBay sellers should focus on products in sweet-spot segments rather than in-season retail. Products that have just hit end-of-life status have been shown to generate the best results on eBay.

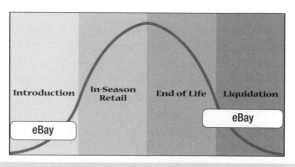

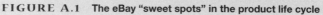

FIGURE A.1 The eBay "sweet spots" in the product life cycle

Understand the eBay Price/Velocity Curve

4

igure A.2 illustrates the eBay price/velocity curve, which shows the relationship between the price you achieve when selling items on eBay versus the volume. The basic premise of the price/velocity curve is that you can sell pretty much anything on eBay, but the price will vary.

From the price/velocity curve, it's important to understand that the more you sell of a certain item, or SKU (short for stock keeping unit), the lower the price you will achieve. If you think about the laws of supply and demand, this makes sense. If demand is constant and you increase supply, the price will decrease.

The top eBay sellers understand the price/velocity curve and by trial and error are able to forecast the amount of a SKU they will be able to sell and the volume they can expect. Being able to forecast the volume and price of your products also helps you when sourcing product. You should be able to buy more volume at a discount and predict how the increased volume will affect your eBay price, so you can have a clear picture of the margin in the product you source before you buy it.

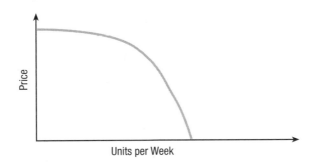

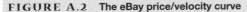

FIGURE A.2 The eBay price/velocity curve

5 Use the Perception-of-Scarcity Strategy

One of the challenges of selling larger volumes (hundreds of items) on eBay is the fact that high-volume listing options such as Dutch auctions or fixed-price auctions reveal the fact that you are selling a large quantity of an item. eBay buyers are very hard-core bargain shoppers, and they are smart enough to realize that when a seller lists 100 of something, they can wait out the seller, because the price will most likely decline.

To counteract this behavior, you can leverage the perception-of-scarcity strategy. There are two components to this strategy:

- **First, take two to four of the items and place them in Buy It Now (BIN) auctions at a price that is 0 to 10% above the average sales price. As these items are sold, be sure to replace them with more BIN items. Some advanced software is available to automate this process for you.**

- **Next, take a portion of inventory (typically 5 to 15%) and auction it off using a very low starting price with no reserve. These auctions will create excitement around the item being sold. Within these auctions, you should link to the BIN auctions.**

When a buyer searches for your item, he will have two choices:

1. **Participate in the low-starting-price, no-reserve auction.**

2. **Buy it now, through one of your BIN listings.**

The "perception of scarcity" creates a call to action for the buyer; typically, most buyers will choose to buy it now. The BIN option also appeals to those buyers who are looking for convenience or are not interested in the competition for the no-reserve auction.

Additionally, once the no-reserve auction ends, one of the bidders will win the item, but the other bidders (which can be a rather large number of people) will still want the item and will be driven to the BIN listings to purchase it.

Sellers who want to move more than 50 items over the course of a month should experiment with the perception-of-scarcity strategy to maximize their yield and velocity.

Use the Second-Chance-Offer Strategy

6

An eBay feature called Second Chance Offer (SCO) was originally created to help with non-paying bidders and reserve auctions. The feature allows the seller to offer an item for sale to the first underbidder (that is, the first bidder who did not win the item). eBay recently expanded the feature to include all underbidders, which has made the SCO very useful as the basis for a pricing strategy.

The SCO strategy works by starting an auction at either a very low price (such as $1.00) or a starting price based on a margin target. Regardless of the starting price, at the end of the auction, the seller can offer the item to all underbidders who bid over a target price.

The benefits of the SCO strategy are substantial:

- **One listing is used to capture multiple buyers.**

- **eBay charges no listing fees for additional SCO sales, resulting in a substantial savings in eBay fees.**

- **There is a perception of scarcity with the SCO strategy, because bidders are not aware when they make a bid that multiple quantities are available.**

- **The seller decides the price threshold at which to extend Second Chance Offers. This allows the seller to manage margin and average selling price.**

- **To accelerate the strategy, promotions can be run for the listing, which will have a positive return on investment, because the cost of the promotions will be shared across many sales rather than just one.**

These benefits make the SCO strategy one of the most powerful available today for maximizing both price and velocity.

7 Optimize Your eBay Search Results

More than 80 million searches are conducted on eBay every day, and more than 80% of eBay buyers locate the items they buy using the eBay search engine. Because buyers focus on using the eBay search engine to locate products, understanding and optimizing how your items are found using the eBay search engine is the single most important promotional step you can take.

The majority of eBay searchers search on "Title only" versus "Title and description." Each eBay listing title has 55 characters, which are indexed by the search engine and displayed as results to the title searches. Thus, it is very important to optimize the 55-character title. In addition to using many keywords in the title, you should also make sure they are the most popular keywords for each item you list. eBay publishes some of the top search terms, and you can also use software that provides detailed traffic analysis, so you can see how buyers are finding your items.

Once titles are optimized, the next important optimization is timing the close of your auctions. Most bids for an item come in the last five to ten minutes. Therefore, it is important to coordinate the closing of your listings with peak eBay traffic times.

A variety of "listing upgrades" are offered by eBay, which may increase the number of buyers who find your items. These upgrades include Subtitle, Bold, Featured Plus, Gift Services, Gallery, and many more. Unfortunately, with most upgrades, the return on investment is not easily measured.

eBay has introduced a program called eBay Keywords that allows a seller to show custom advertisements based on specific search terms. The best part of the program is that you pay only when a potential buyer clicks on the advertisement (a system called "pay per click"). The eBay Keywords program provides complete data on the traffic delivered, allowing you to measure the success of your advertising. More generally, this type of advertising, in which you pay only when a buyer takes an action, is known as "pay for performance."

Build Your eBay Brand

8

The top sellers on eBay have created strong eBay brands. In addition to a business name and a logo, your eBay brand is the sum of many parts, such as the category in which you sell, any special promotions you offer, and more.

The first step to building a great eBay brand is to design a professional-looking design for your listings. eBay offers basic listing templates and an HTML designer. Other software and services are also available to help you improve the professionalism of your listings.

Next, you should look at creating a custom, professional "About Me" page. eBay traffic analysis suggests that many buyers go to the page both to find out more about a seller and to find more items for sale by the seller. A strong About Me page can significantly improve sales.

Finally, we recommend that you open an eBay Store, with a professional design that ties in to the look of your listings and your About Me page.

Additionally, if you have any other interaction with buyers—such as specialized e-mails, checkouts, or an e-commerce site for add-on sales—reinforce your brand at every point of contact.

9 Explore Other Channels

With more than 100 million shoppers, eBay represents one of the largest channels on the Internet. However, there will come a time when you reach a plateau on eBay or when your business becomes large enough that you need to diversify a little. Also, you may want to expand outside of the eBay "sweet spots" and into in-season retail, for example.

There are many other channels you can explore besides eBay. Based on the success of other sellers, we recommend the following options.

- **Yahoo! Stores.** Now formally called Yahoo! Small Business Merchant Solutions (YSBMS, for short), this is a quick and relatively inexpensive way to create your own e-commerce site that is hosted and powered by Yahoo!.

- **Amazon.com.** Amazon.com has numerous offerings for sellers. We recommend trying the Amazon Marketplace.

- **Your own e-commerce site.** One of the top additional channels you should explore is having your own e-commerce site.

The leading promotional vehicles for e-commerce sites are these:

- **Search engines/portals.** Search engines such as Yahoo! and Google are the starting point for many Internet purchases. You can either optimize your site for the algorithmic portion of the search engine or pay for placement in the "sponsored links" portion of most sites.

- **Shopping engines.** Within most portals are shopping engines. Many buyers use these engines—either on a portal or at the engine's independent site—to choose an e-commerce site. Outside of the portals (such as Yahoo! Shopping, Shop@AOL, and MSN Shopping), there are independent popular shopping engines, such as Shopping.com, mySimon.com, and PriceGrabber.com

- **Affiliate programs.** Another successful promotional tool for e-commerce is an affiliate program. With such programs, you agree to share your revenue with Web site owners who send buyers to you.

- **E-mail newsletters.** Given the investment you will make to acquire online customers, one of the best ways to maximize that investment is to provide a high-quality e-mail newsletter to every customer who wants one.

Use an eBay Dashboard 10

A dashboard is a one-page report that provides the current eBay vital statistics for your business as well as the trends over the last several periods. We suggest an eBay dashboard that includes such eBay vital statistics as gross merchandise sales, average sales price, conversion rate, and margin.

The most effective eBay dashboard not only captures the vital signs, but also shows a trend over several periods. We recommend tracking the last four weeks of data (about a month's worth) so you can see short-term and longer-term trends. Additionally, you may want to consider tracking the last three months' worth of data (a quarterly view) and the last 12 months' or four quarters' worth of data (an annual view).

We recommend four more dashboards for sellers who want to track the complete performance of their eBay business and implement the Five P's strategic framework introduced in this book:

- **Product dashboard.** The product dashboard allows you to see the vital statistics for every SKU, such as the SKU's average sales price, conversion rate, margin, and so on. Based on this information, you can make smarter sourcing decisions and develop better product sales strategies.

- **Price dashboard.** Like the product dashboard, the price dashboard presents information for every SKU. But instead of product information, the price dashboard presents the pricing strategy and pricing results for the SKU. This information allows you to measure the impact of your price strategies on your business.

- **Promotion dashboard.** The promotion dashboard illustrates the impact your promotional activities are having on your business by showing the changes in traffic. You can also optionally look at promotion on a SKU-by-SKU basis. Additionally, we recommend tracking the top search terms, so you can use the information in the eBay Keywords program and to optimize the titles of your listings.

- **Placement dashboard.** For eBay businesses that sell on multiple channels in addition to eBay, a placement dashboard will allow you to see how the various channels are performing. Important metrics for the placement dashboard are each channel's gross merchandise sales, average sales price, conversion rate, marketplace fees, and take rate.

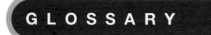

$NR eBay seller slang for a listing that starts at $1.00 with no reserve. Sometimes you see $1NR, as well.

active user An eBay term, denoting a registered user who has bid, bought, or sold in the last 12 months.

affiliate program A promotional program in which you offer revenue shares to other Web sites so that they will promote your products across the Internet.

attach ASP The average selling price for items that are attached as a secondary item onto a primary purchase.
Formula: up-sold GMS ÷ up-sold items

attach rate   For checkout systems that support up-selling, the rate at which customers are up-sold, or at which they attach to the original order.
Formula: items up-sold per month ÷ total items sold

average order value (AOV)   The average value of orders, which is useful if you are consolidating orders (that is, allowing more than one item per order).
Formula: GMS ÷ number of orders

average sales price (ASP)   The average sales price over a period of time.
Formula: GMS ÷ number of sales = ASP

BIN rate   The percentage of items sold that are attributable to the BIN and fixed-price formats.
Formula: BIN/FP items sold ÷ total items sold

conversion rate (CR)   The pace at which your listed items are selling, expressed as a percentage.
Formula: number of items listed ÷ number of items sold

dashboard   A one-page report that, like the dashboard of a car, gives you all the information you need to drive your eBay business.

deadbeat   On eBay, a buyer who bids on an item but fails to complete the transaction, by not paying. Also known as a non-paying bidder (NPB).

eBay Keywords   A new program eBay has introduced that allows sellers to place banner ads strategically in response to eBay buyer searches.

Five P's   Easy-to-remember mnemonic for the eBay business strategic framework. The Five P's are product, price, promotion, placement, and performance.

flame out   eBay seller slang for when an eBay business goes out of business.

gross merchandise sales (GMS)   The volume of your sales on eBay.

items per order (IPO)   The number of items per order, which is useful if you are consolidating orders. *Formula: number of items ÷ number of orders*

margin   The ultimate cash generated by your business, sometimes called net income, the bottom line, or profit.

multi-channel   Term used to describe your business when you go from one channel (eBay is typically first) to many online channels (at least two).

new in box (NIB)   eBay slang for an item that is new and in its original box.

new with tags (NWT)   eBay slang for a new clothing item that comes with the original tags still attached.

no reserve (NR)   An auction listing that has no reserve price.

non-paying bidder (NPB)   See **deadbeat**.

not a registered user (NARU)   eBay slang for a seller who has been kicked off the marketplace.

pay for performance (P4P)   An Internet marketing vehicle in which you pay only when an action takes place. For example, paying when a user clicks on your ad.

pay per click (PPC)   Paid-search programs in which you pay only when a potential buyer clicks on your listing or advertisement.

price/velocity curve   A curve that shows the relationship between the price you achieve for your goods and the volume you are able to sell over an amount of time. As volume, or velocity, increases, prices tend to come down. Alternatively, you can achieve higher prices by decreasing the velocity.

product life cycle   As new products are released, they mature through a well-defined product life cycle. The four phases of the product life cycle are introduction, in-season retail, end of life, and liquidation.

registered users   The total number of registered accounts on eBay.

return on investment (ROI)   To marketing professionals, the return on advertising spending. For example, if you spend $200 on promotions that drive $2,000 in additional sales, you have an ROI of 10. In other words, you received ten times the value of your initial investment in return.

S+H margin   The margin (or loss) made on shipping and handling, expressed as both an absolute value and a percentage.

search engine marketing (SEM)   The service performed by companies that manage search advertising.

search engine optimization (SEO)   Service performed by a company that will "tweak" your Web site so that it shows up higher in the algorithmic portion of search engine results.

Second Chance Offer (SCO)   An eBay feature that allows a seller to make offers to under-bidders for the amount they bid on an item. Typically used for reserve auctions and NPB situations, SCO can also be used to accelerate velocity as the foundation of a pricing strategy.

sniping   Sniping occurs when a buyer places a winning bid in the last minutes or seconds of an auction. Smart eBay buyers almost exclusively use sniping as a buying strategy, and numerous software applications for automating sniping are available.

stock keeping unit (SKU)   An individual, unique inventory item.

take rate (TR)   The amount, expressed as a percentage, of your GMS that goes toward eBay fees.
Formula: TR = eBay fees ÷ GMS

total payment accounts   The number of registered PayPal accounts.

total payment volume (TPV)   The transactional volume that goes through PayPal in a given time frame.

unpaid items (UPI)   New term used to describe an item that has a winning bidder, but for which the winning bidder did not pay. See also **deadbeat**.

INDEX

competition (*continued*)
  price pressure, 12
  researching, 104–105
  with self, 103
CompUSA, as product source, 88
Computers category
  ASP decrease, 104
  buyer behavior, 103–104
  GMS run rate, 9
consolidating orders
  calculating average order
    value, 34–35
  items per order ratio, 34–35
Consumer Electronics category,
  9
convenience buyers, 112, 113,
  117, 124, 260
conversion rate (CR)
  calculating, 35
  defined, 11, 53
  eBay average, 40
  estimated range, 11
  examples, 36
  gross *vs.* net, 36
  including on dashboards, 223,
    226, 229
  overview, 35–36
  and take rate, 44–45, 46
  tracking SKUs, 229
  as vital sign, 35–36
  what-if scenarios, 41–42
cost per click (CPC), 153, 163, 165
CrazyApe case study, 205–210
customer service. *See also* feedback
  CrazyApe example, 210
  feedback as indicator, 47

including on dashboards, 223,
  228
UrbanImport example, 263

D

dashboards. *See also* performance
  annual, 221–222
  defined, 252
  downloading sample, 253
  including vital signs, 222–224
  JustDeals example, 249–250
  monthly, 221
  for non-eBay channels, 242–245
  overview, 220–222, 277
  placement-related, 242–245
  price-related, 235–238
  product-related, 229–234
  promotion-related, 238–242
  quarterly, 221
  samples, 225–228, 231–234,
    236–238, 240–242, 243–245
  summary, 277
  weekly, 221, 222
deadbeats. *See* non-paying bidders (NPBs)
deals of the day/week/month,
  173–174
demand. *See* supply and demand
depth, product, 79–82
DesignerAthletic case study,
  126–131
digital cameras
  Canon PowerShot S400 exam-
    ple, 13–15
  competition example, 12–13
discount bins, as product source,
  87

multi-channel strategy (*continued*)

    summary, 204, 276

    tracking performance on dashboards, 242–245

    UrbanImport example, 263–264

    when to use, 192–193

multi-seller-ID strategy, 188–189

mySimon, 190, 201, 208, 216

N

narrow categories, 82–84

NARU (not a registered user), 16–17, 23

net conversion rate, 36

net margin, 50–51

newsletters, e-mail

    CrazyApe example, 209

    as e-commerce site strategy, 215

    e-mail overview, 203–204

    as eBay seller strategy, 176

    Web links, 216

NexTag, 201, 217

Nokia, 90

non-paying bidders (NPBs), 31. *See also* NPB rate

Nortica e-Bay 500, 9

not a registered user (NARU), 16–17, 23

NPB rate

    computing, 32

    defined, 32, 53

    tracking on dashboard, 223, 230

O

one-day listings, 187

open-box returns, 18

opt-in newsletters

    CrazyApe example, 209

    as e-commerce site strategy, 215

    as eBay seller strategy, 176

    overview, 203–204

    Web links, 216

oversourcing, 82

Overstockb2b.com, as product source, 89

Overstock.com, 105

oversupply, market, 77, 80

Overture/Yahoo!

    advertising effectiveness, 138

    paid search, 152, 154, 199, 216

    and product life cycle, 190

P

packing materials. *See* S+H margin

paid search

    Google example, 200–201

    JustDeals example, 247, 249

    overview, 198–201

    summary, 204

    Web links, 216

    Yahoo! example, 199–200

Palm PDAs

    perception-of-scarcity example, 115–116

    self-competition example, 103

pass-through costs, 47

pay per click (PPC), 198, 211. *See also* paid search

Disabled Online Users Association
Self-sufficiency through selling on eBay

The Disabled Online Users Association assists the differently-abled in becoming self sufficient through selling on eBay. This is accomplished through a grassroots effort of the online selling community who generously volunteer their time, talents and resources. Each qualified student is assigned a mentor to teach them the skills necessary to become an independent and successful seller on eBay. Having found their wings, many of our students become mentors themselves and continue to "pay it forward." Today DOUA has a community base of over 500 students, mentors, volunteers and supporters.

informIT

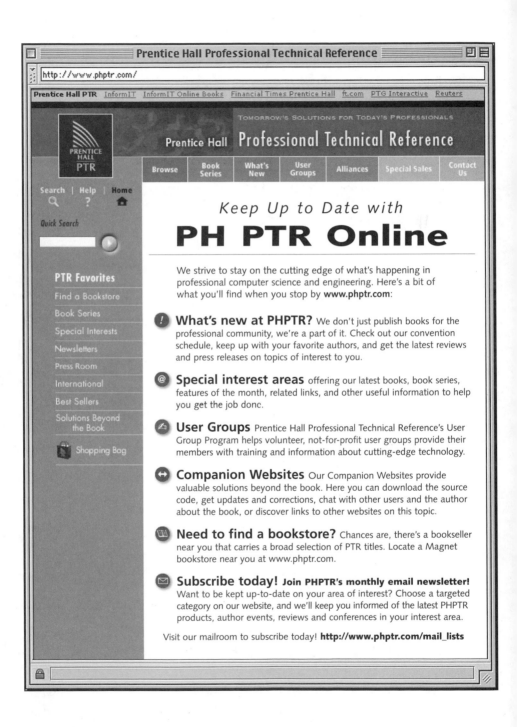